The Enigma of Economic Growth

David Horowitz

The Praeger Special Studies program—utilizing the most modern and efficient book production techniques and a selective worldwide distribution network—makes available to the academic, government, and business communities significant, timely research in U.S. and international economic, social, and political development.

The Enigma of Economic Growth

A Case Study of Israel

Praeger Publishers   New York   Washington   London

PRAEGER SPECIAL STUDIES IN INTERNATIONAL ECONOMICS AND DEVELOPMENT

PRAEGER PUBLISHERS
111 Fourth Avenue, New York, N.Y. 10003, U.S.A.
5, Cromwell Place, London S.W.7, England

Published in the United States of America in 1972
by Praeger Publishers, Inc.

Second printing, 1974

All rights reserved

© 1972 by Praeger Publishers, Inc.

Library of Congress Catalog Card Number: 77-184338

Printed in the United States of America

CONTENTS

	Page
LIST OF TABLES	viii
INTRODUCTION	xi

PART I: CONDITIONS AND EFFECTS
OF TRANSPLANTATION

Chapter

1	THE INTERNATIONAL AND HISTORICAL BACK-GROUND	3
	Notes	14
2	ECONOMIC GROWTH: STIMULATING AND RE-TARDING FACTORS	15
	Demography	15
	Scarcity of Natural Resources	19
	The Geopolitical Situation	19
	The Transformation of Agriculture	20
	Industrialization	30
	Construction	37
	Notes	38
3	STANDARD OF LIVING AND INCOME DISTRIBUTION	39
	Note	48
4	CAPITAL INFLUX AND CAPITAL FORMATION	49
	Capital and Economic Growth	49
	The Role of Public Capital	53
	Capital Formation and Savings	55
	Structural Changes of the Economy	57
	Notes	62

Chapter   Page

5   HUMAN AND NATURAL RESOURCES AND ECO-
     NOMIC GROWTH   65

          The Human Factor in the Development of Israel   65
          Capacity of Absorption   70
          Notes   75

6   ECONOMIC GROWTH AND THE MECHANICS OF
     TRANSPLANTATION   77

          Notes   87

                    PART II: PATTERNS AND POLICIES

     Introduction to Part II   91

7   ECONOMIC POLICY   95

          The Targets and Ingredients of Economic Policy
             in Israel   95
          Monetary Policy   105
          Fiscal Policy   107
          Conclusions   110
          Note   112

8   SOCIOECONOMIC POLYMORPHIA   113

          Note   118

9   THE BALANCE OF PAYMENTS   119

10   THE WAR ECONOMY   127

          Effects of Political and Military Events on
             Israel's Economy   127
          The Administered Areas   132
          Note   135

11   THE NEW PATTERN   137

          Developments in Israel's Economy   139
          The Shift to Sophisticated and Science-Based
             Industries   142
          Observations   143
          Note   144

Chapter   Page

12   THE ENIGMA OF ECONOMIC GROWTH: SUMMARY
      AND CONCLUSIONS   145

ABOUT THE AUTHOR   159

LIST OF TABLES

Table		Page
1	Key Indicators of Economic Development in Palestine, Selected Years, 1922-38	6
2	Key Indicators of Economic Development, 1950-70	8
3	Generation and Sales of Electricity, 1950-69	8
4	Net Domestic Product and National Income at Factor Cost, by Economic Branch, 1952, 1960, and 1969	21
5	FAO Country Index Numbers of Per Capita Total Agricultural Production, 1968	25
6	Key Indicators of Economic Growth, 1952, 1960, and 1970	27
7	Change in Average Yields of Selected Crops, 1955-69	28
8	Exports of Agricultural Products, 1960-70	28
9	Indicators of Growth in Factory Production, 1950, 1960, and 1969	31
10	Net Output of Industry by Main Branches, 1950, 1960, and 1970	35
11	Growth in Ownership of Electric Appliances and Private Cars	40
12	Breakdown of Average Expenditure of Wage-Earner's Family, Selected Years, 1956/57-1968/69	42
13	Gross Monetary Income Per Adult, Selected Years, 1957/58-1968/69	43
14	Coefficient of Inequality in Gross Income in Israel, 1967-70	45
15	Income Distribution Among Total Population Based on Tax Data, Selected Countries	46
16	Breakdown of Labor Force by Economic Branch, 1955, 1960, 1966, and 1969	59

Table   Page

17   Literacy and School Attendance in Selected Countries   67

18   Increase in Means of Payment in Selected Countries,
        Annual Average for the Years 1950-69   103

19   Composition of the Government Budget for 1970-71,
        by Main Categories   108

20   Contributions of Foreign Currency Accruals to State
        Budget, 1963-64, 1966-67, and 1970-71   109

21   Net Domestic Product and Employment, by Sector,
        Selected Years, 1953-60   117

22   Indexes of Import, Export, and Import of Capital Goods,
        1950-70   121

23   Exports of Goods, by Main Groups, 1961 and 1970   124

24   Exports of Services, by Main Groups, 1961 and 1970   124

25   Growth of Real Total and Per Capita Consumption,
        1967-70   129

26   Money Supply, 1967-70   129

27   GNP and Resources in the Administered Areas,
        1968-70   134

28   Product Growth in Selected Countries, 1954-64   140

29   International Comparison on Growth Rates of Aggre-
        gate and Per Capita Product in the 1960's   141

ix

Israel is a small country and, at first sight, the vicissitudes of its development appear of little significance on the broader horizons of economic thought and analysis. And yet, many of the most important trends and problems of modern economics are vividly reflected within this microcosm. The very smallness of the entity lightens the task of tracing the sequence of events and discerning the interplay of forces. The problems of cyclical fluctuations, of the impact of modern industrialization, of an occupational reshuffle, of the transition to an exchange economy—all these are reproduced and magnified as though in an experimental laboratory. In this miniature form, changes and trends become more transparent, and generalizations may be reached of possible concern to the economics of growth as a whole.

The question is whether, by an analysis of the conditions of this experiment in transplantation of population and in economic growth, the wider rules and mechanics of such processes can be ascertained and defined, whether there is anything that can be termed the mechanics of transplantation, governed by rules of all-embracing validity and influence in this context.

Israel's venture stands out against that background and offers a line of empirical approach to such problems as population pressure, migration, and economic absorption. Therefore, an attempt will be made here to use Israel as a test case for certain problems of economic growth.

The processes of population transplantation and of economic growth take place in Israel under exceptional conditions, a fact that may to some extent simplify the analysis and dissection of their components and the measuring of their weights, thereby simplifying the task of discovering rules that could be of general validity.

The comparatively circumscribed scope and area of Israel throw the various factors into bold relief and in that way its development sheds light not only on the theoretical problems of economic absorption of population and economic growth but also on the practical problems of migration, so that an analysis of the past record of economic growth, particularly in the years 1950-70, may provide a key to the explanation of some of them.

During those two decades, Israel underwent an unprecedented economic expansion: the curve of economic activity rose steeply and the pace of development was unusually rapid. This phenomenon in an area of a few thousand square miles can only be explained by some peculiar array of circumstances. The crucial issue is whether it has its source in external or in internal conditions, although obviously each category of conditions reacts on the other and their inter-ratios are constantly changing.

Exogenous extra-economic factors play an exceptionally large role in the development of Israel. Geopolitical and strategic conjunctures, the historical background, psychological and ideological forces, and ethnic diversity are among the most powerful determinants of Israel's social and economic pattern, and no analysis of its formation and growth can afford to disregard them.

The political background especially must always be kept in mind. Political events exert a much more decisive influence on Israel's economy than is usual in other countries, owing to the special role of immigration and capital import, and regional events and developments. Two sets of forces shape the political background—forces that repel Jewish communities and capital from their countries of domicile and induce them to turn to Israel for refuge and forces that lend Israel its magnetism as a sanctuary for them. These forces of repulsion and attraction often are sufficiently strong to outweigh and override the effect of internal conditions. Their impact throws into sharp relief the pattern of economic growth peculiar to Israel, which is very different from that of other developing countries.

The first United Nations Development Decade saw only meager contributions to change in the economic conditions and pattern of the Third World. Although the pace of annual growth in the underdeveloped nations was slightly faster than that of the developed nations (5.0 percent as opposed to 4.8 percent), the rise in per capita output was in reverse ratio (2.5 percent as opposed to 3.6 percent), reflecting the population explosion in the developing nations, which cancelled out and neutralized the effects of their swifter economic growth.

The report of the World Bank for the year 1964-65 registered exceptions to this general trend, listing as deviating from the overall pattern and distinguished by an exceptional rate of economic growth Taiwan and Thailand in Asia; Tunisia and Libya in Africa; Israel and Iraq in the Middle East; Greece, Spain, and Yugoslavia in Southern Europe; and Mexico, Peru, and Venezuela in Latin America.

A World Bank mission that spent several weeks in Israel in October-November 1968 had this to say about Israel's economic growth:

Israel's past economic performance has been remarkable. Against great odds such as a conspicuous dearth of natural resources, hostile neighbours and the need to provide a large inflow of immigrants with housing and other facilities, real GNP has been growing at an average annual rate of some 10 percent since 1950 while per capita production increased by an average of 5 percent. These achievements were largely the result of two factors: a capable and determined population with a broad base of well-educated and energetic people who proved able to overcome the difficulties of economic development with great ingenuity; and a relatively large and continuous flow of foreign capital originating chiefly from private donations of American Jews and from reparation payments by West Germany. Israel's "economic miracle" would have been impossible if one of these growth factors—human skill and foreign capital—had been lacking.

Thus, although the circumstances have been abnormal, it should be rewarding to analyze the economic progress in Israel over the years 1950-70 as a case study that might justify effectual economic generalizations and theoretical conclusions of some universality with regard to the conditions of rapid economic growth. This is the purpose of the present study, based on statistical and research material assembled in Israel and on the author's personal experience.

Judged by its natural resources, Israel is poor: it has no oil, no coal, no ores, and no timber; its water supply is limited; two-thirds of its land area consists of desert and barren hills that can be transformed only by arduous toil and the infusion of science and capital.

Israel's economic dependence on world conditions, on the stimulants of import of capital and population, and on geography is unique and adds greatly to the difficulty of isolating its development and reaching universal conclusions and generalizations. This is reflected in a statement surveying the economy of Mandated Palestine:

Palestine is probably the least self-contained country in the world. Its destiny is governed more by unpredictable political events elsewhere than by predictable economic events within its frontiers. The "racial" policy of Germany since 1933; the Italo-Ethiopian conflict of 1935-36; the Spanish civil war of 1936; the dissolution of the gold block in 1936; the re-armament policies of European and American States in 1935-36—all these have a far more important effect on the movement of capital and labor to Palestine than the attractions and repulsions of local events in the country itself.*

---

*Government of Palestine, Department of Migration, Annual Report, 1936, p. 21.

The problem had already been recognized and correctly evaluated by the Mandatory:

> The effective question to which no effective answer can yet be returned is concerned, in Palestine, with the possibility of relating human intelligence to the material resources in such a way that increasing production of subsistence for the population can keep pace with the growth of the population itself. A population depends for its subsistence on what it can acquire by its own efforts applied to the natural resources. *

Notwithstanding these important and enlightening assessments, the period of the Mandatory Administration cannot be covered in detail in this study, for several reasons: (1) the delimitation of frontiers is so different now that no solid basis of comparison exists; (2) the legislative framework and economic pattern of the period were so dissimilar that they do not lend themselves to any worthwhile apposition; and (3) dependable statistics for the period are lacking. Therefore, references to the period of the Mandatory Administration will be included only as far as they are germane to the present, suggest the source in that earlier period of current trends and developments, or may be regarded as predicting current tendencies in the light of our understanding of fundamental features in the economies of both Palestine and Israel.

Moreover, the study will confine itself, largely, to the last two decades, virtually omitting the years 1948-1949 and their cataclysmic fluctuations, when 10 percent of the population were in transit camps and the statistical service had only begun. Anyhow, the period from 1950 to 1970 is the decisive one for our purpose.

---

*Government of Palestine, Census of Palestine, 1931, Vol. I, Part 1, pp. 46, 252.

CONDITIONS
AND EFFECTS
OF
TRANSPLANTATION

In the economic situation of the interwar period, rapid immigration, creating a home market, offered distinct possibilities of reproducing the conditions of an economy of growth. Prices of primary products declined more as a result of the world crisis than did prices of secondary products because the readjustment of the manufacturing industry to a contraction of markets is easier, smoother, and faster than that of farming.[1]

Thus, for a new country to embark on producing primary products for export became feasible only under exceptionally favorable conditions since world markets were overloaded with the dead weight of surplus stocks from almost every nation.

In the past, colonies began by producing foods and raw materials. Obviously, a new country with a small home market cannot begin with secondary production but must concentrate on primary: "Countries started with something to sell."[2]

In the interwar period, the greatest and most typical difficulty was to ensure sufficient purchasing power to absorb the flood of commodities pouring from factory and field. Thus, migration based exclusively on the production of primary commodities for the world market could not be successful. Again and again, economic growth was halted because of this marketing problem. After World War I, New Zealand settled its ex-servicemen on the land and set them to growing fruit, but they grew more than they could sell and the country lost heavily.[3]

The report to the Secretary of State for Dominion Affairs of the Inter-Departmental Committee on Migration Policy, presented to Parliament in August 1934, described the problem for developing countries:

> There should be a reasonably secure and available
> market for a considerable proportion of the produce of
> the migrant's labour, and the question of whether such
> a market exists or can be developed is . . . the first
> criterion which should be applied to every scheme of
> migration of every kind. . . .
>
> Indeed it is obvious that the moment that the needs
> of the individual include commodities which he cannot
> himself produce, he must be able to sell what he can
> produce if he is to be able to procure what he cannot
> produce. And inasmuch as the newcomer in any com-
> munity, either because he has to create new markets
> for his produce, or to compete with neighbours longer
> established than himself, in existing markets which may
> already be fully supplied, is always likely to meet with
> difficulty, at any rate at first, in disposing of his pro-
> duce, these considerations apply with particular force
> to the migrant. . . .
>
> In healthy conditions of trade and exchange it may
> well be that there is a latent demand which will become
> or can be made actual with increased production. More-
> over, it must not be overlooked that the mere fact of
> settlement and the initial expenditure of capital in the
> country of settlement will of itself tend to create the con-
> ditions in which an increased supply can be marketed; in
> other words the settlers themselves contribute in some
> degree towards the creation of the market for their own
> commodities.

Moreover,

> . . . migrants must, if they are to live, be able to sell
> what they produce in order to buy what they need. . . .
>
> Whereas in the past supply, generally speaking,
> has always lagged behind demand, it is now clear that
> it is possible so rapidly and so greatly to increase the
> supply of almost any commodity that there will be a con-
> stant prospect of supply overtaking demand. [4]

It is evident that, owing to a dearth of marketing prospects in the interwar period, agricultural settlement, as such and alone, did

not effectually prove itself. The safety valve of migration was almost
shut by a braking of the quantitative and structural growth of mature
Western economies and of the rapid population rises in the developed
countries which, in the past, had stimulated an ever brisker demand
for primary products—foodstuffs as well as raw materials. Since
no market could now be found for these, settlement on conventional
lines was doomed in advance. The interwar slowing down of expansion
in the mature Western capitalist economies blocked an outlet for
colonization similar to that in the nineteenth century, which was based
on primary production for world markets. That is why, for example,
attempts at agricultural settlement in Manchuria and Italian Africa
did not succeed. The failure can hardly be attributed to want of space
or exhaustion of natural resources. Rather, the explanation is to be
found in international economic conditions and in the difficulties of
marketing new products: these factors apparently account for immigration to areas that already have a considerable concentration of
population. The decline in world trade and the virtual saturation of
markets for primary commodities make it extremely difficult to
transplant a population by dint of agricultural settlement and the production of such commodities.

This state of affairs does not appear to have been subjected to
any radical change by World War II and its aftermath. A plethora of
raw materials and primary commodities is piled up in producing
countries and all the signs suggest that this is a long-term trend.
These conditions lead to pessimistic estimates of settlement possibilities, as the actual and potential production of raw materials and
foodstuffs precludes this possibility. [5]

Thus, the knowledge that the process of development on the
pattern of the nineteenth century was terminated by a radical change
of conditions determined the evaluation of the possibilities and prospects for migratory movements. [6]

On the face of it, Israel would seem an exception to this general
experience since immigration and economic expansion went on continuously. The indexes shown in Table 1, taken from all economic
spheres, summarize and mirror the correlations among absorption
of immigrants, rapid economic growth, the broadening of the economic base, and the dynamic expansion of the entire economy.

Comparison with similar ventures in the same interwar period
shows that Israel's development was sui generis although ventures
not unlike it, if slower paced, were tried in other parts of the world,
particularly in the nineteenth century. This divergence, marking
the transplantation of Greeks from Asia Minor to Greece, which took
place during the early 1920s, calls for a theoretical explanation.

TABLE 1

Key Indicators of Economic Development in
Palestine, Selected Years, 1922-38
(absolute figures per capita of settled population)

	1922	1925	1928-30	1937-38
Gross production industry and agriculture[a]	LP[c] 5,705	7,300	9,528	14,975
Consumption of commodities	LP[c] 8,500	10,940	12,800	15,700
Main capital investments	LP[c] 47,000	53,500	70,800	105,700
Energy used (billions of kilocalories per thousand inhabitants)	0.8	0.8	1.4	1.8
Total Jewish population of which: new immigrants[b]	84,000 —	122,000 31,000	175,000 60,000	437,000 279,000

[a]Price basis: 1937.
[b]Post-1922 immigrants.
[c]Palestinian pounds equal to pounds sterling and convertible into pounds sterling.

6

Palestine, like Greece, was not a venture of colonization following the traditional pattern but, rather, the scene of a transplantation of population. This took the form of a transfer in sudden undulations of an immigrant population possessing the prerequisites of skill and capital and automatically providing its own internal market. The process requires an artificial noneconomic driving power, a quick movement of people condensed within a short space of time. Its structural character is different from forms of settlement that aim at producing primary commodities, particularly foodstuffs, for the world market. It is based on effective internal demand synthesized within the country itself by imports of capital and manpower that provide an adequate substitute for export markets. The reference, of course, is to real demand generated by an influx of capital and the growth of the GNP, not by inflation and an artificial and fleeting expansion of purchasing power that exceeds real resources.

Table 2 presents indicators of the economic growth for the period 1950-70, which was even more impressive than that during the Mandatory period.

Another indicator of economic growth is the consumption of electric power, particularly for irrigation and industry, which registers the expansion of production, side by side with indexes of contemporaneous population growth in two decades (see Table 3).

In an epoch that saw a general falling off in migration and the failure of major colonization enterprises, Greeks were transplanted from Asia Minor and Jews transplanted to Palestine without dislocation of the economic life of either country.

Transplantation, if it is accompanied by occupational redistribution and population restratification, opens a home market, and the importance of that as preconditioning any shift of population has been emphasized by recent economic developments: "Markets are more important than raw materials and capital."[7] The problem of effective demand is partly solved by the very act of transplantation, in particular at the beginning, by the lag of production behind expanding consumption and by concurrent investment of capital. The lag, in turn, is an incentive and stimulus of expanding production, driving manpower into its orbit. There appears the replica, as it were, of a growing population and a larger market which are familiar from the period of colonization, with this difference; the growing population in the metropolitan, developed countries then constituted the expanding market, whereas transplantation enlarges the local market, thereby eliminating the gravest obstacle in the way of economic expansion, namely, the intermittent sluggishness of effective demand.

TABLE 2

Key Indicators of Economic Development,
1950-70

	1950	1970	Index of Change (1950 = 100)
GNP per capita (IL of 1955)	865	2, 684	310
Private consumption per capita (IL of 1955)	734	1, 799	245
Public consumption per capita (IL of 1955)	217	782	360
Gross domestic capital formation per capita (IL of 1955)	478	627	131
Average population (thousands)	1, 267	2, 957	234
New immigrants*	666	1, 143	172

*Since May 15, 1948.

TABLE 3

Generation and Sales of Electricity, 1950-69

	1950	1960	1969
Installed generating capacity (mw)	100	410	1, 012
Generation (million kwh)	543	2, 205	5, 903
Sales, total (million kwh)	464	1, 857	5, 068
To industry (million kwh)	141	669	1, 715
To agriculture (million kwh)	117	430	1, 187
Other sales (million kwh)	206	758	2, 166
Number of consumers (thousands)	179	551	882
Population (thousands)	1, 267	2, 117	1, 879

Some aspects of the problem were recognized by Paul Mombert:

This connection is seen even more clearly if account if taken of the influence of the size of the population on demand, and through demand on production. Technical progress can be exploited for economic purposes only with the achievement of mass production which is impossible without mass consumption. [8]

Therefore, the fact that in Palestine, and afterward in Israel, consumption outran production goes far toward explaining the swift development. Surplus capital was available and ready to seize any opportunity for investment, if only a market could be assured. An intensive flow of immigration, endowed with a sufficiency of imported purchasing power, gave the assurance, and at once capital began producing, by large-scale investment, to meet the demand.

The success of transplantation from Asia Minor to Greece is no doubt susceptible of similar explanation. Sir John Hope Simpson records that Greece, small and impoverished though it was, rapidly integrated, into areas already densely settled, a number of newcomers equal to one-third of its population at the time. [9]

It will be asked whether transfers of population contribute to higher productivity and better economic interrelations that result in a higher standard of living. This point may be viewed from two angles:

1. The relation between the population added to a certain area and the resources of that area, and the approximation to an optimum of productivity under the new conditions brought about by demographic shift and transplantation. Migration in the era of free movement of capital, goods, and men was determined chiefly by the relation of population to resources and the shift from areas of higher to areas of lower demographic pressure. The solitary exceptions were migrations dictated and engendered by political and religious persecutions or such exceptional circumstances as the Irish famine. This issue must be analyzed by the method of interspatial and intertemporal comparisons, the level of productivity, the consumption and standard of living of a given territory, and can be resolved on the basis of indexes referring to it.

2. A consideration of movements of population as such, viz., from the angle of the economic effects of transplantation.

The favorable or adverse outcome of a population transfer depends upon the existing economic structure. If at that juncture markets are contracting and productivity is rising, it is very probable that, with the resultant disparity between production and purchasing power, the transfer will make for a sounder equilibrium and improved standards of living. This seems to be borne out by the experience of Greece and Palestine, and even more by that of Israel, where a diversified economic structure was so quickly created by transplantation; transplantation so conditioned reproduces new marketing possibilities since the immigrants abandon capital, equipment, housing, and so forth in one country and must reestablish them in another.

Another aspect of the problem is underlined by Jens Warmings in a diagram that shows how wages depend upon the number of workers; his paradoxical conclusion is "that the total wealth of the world would increase if people migrated from one country to another."[10]

At the Hot Springs Conference, which deliberated on the refugee problem immediately after World War II, the United States delegation submitted a memorandum envisaging mass postwar movements of population to secure an evener distribution of supplies, movements that would involve the emigration of surplus workers, internal resettlement, and the shifting of farm labor to factories, or a combination of all three processes. It is significant that, in Greece and Palestine and afterward in Isreal, the upshot of transplantation was to strengthen the trend from primary to secondary and tertiary stages of production and the process of urbanization.

In the economic development of Palestine and Israel only the starting step—citriculture—had production for the world market as its aim. Production for the home market was soon dominant. This changeover was accelerated by the building movement, which set economic activity alight and eased the absorption of immigrants. The sudden expansion of the home market, coupled with the import of capital and manpower which intensified demand, promoted the establishment and proliferation of the machinery of production. At a subsequent stage of development, in a more mature economy, this trend has been reversed.

Thus, transplantation produced the exceptional circumstances in which such a structural economic growth became possible by simulating the expansion of demand similar to that which a managed economy can contrive when resort is had to pump-priming—armament activity or large-scale bolstering of the market by official intervention—always provided that the expansion is real and is generated by influx of capital and growth of the GNP.

The proportion of immigrants to population both in Palestine and in Isreal has been high, particularly in the first years of the state, and immigration has had an economic moment transcending its absolute numbers. Therefore, the influence of immigration on economic development must have been very pronounced. Indeed, at the beginning it was the principal determining force in the economy. Even today, when an autonomous economic organism has come into being, an organism in some degree subject to internal fluctuations of boom and depression, the swelling or slackening of immigration may be sufficiently powerful to obscure or to stress the usual ups and downs that otherwise, in all likelihood, would make themselves distinctly felt.

World War II witnessed more than one transplantation; tremendous deployments of troops from one area to another, flights of refugees, uprootings of population. The gigantic scope and feverish speed of the action seem to be the essentials of success. Transplantation is the very opposite of infiltration and its modalities are different.

But that transplantation provides the foundation for an economy of mounting numbers would not in itself be enough to guarantee economic expansion. It is indispensable that there be capital to develop the natural resources of the country of absorption and its processing industries, which do not depend on natural resources, and an initial financing of what all who are employed in the investment sector must consume.

Developing countries must compete for capital with highly developed industrial ones. The competition is tough, and to succeed requires most propitious circumstances. Israel was guaranteed a steady influx of capital of no little magnitude. This transplanted capital fertilized and developed Israel's economy. It was an artificial diversion of capital for noneconomic reasons, the result of what is called co-migration, that is, immigration linked with capital import, the two running parallel but not always simultaneous. Thus, the advantage of a plentiful and continuing supply of capital that Israel enjoys stemmed in the main from the special conditions of the world Jewish population.

The import of some $10 billion of capital in two decades is not unique. Where Israel's development diverges from that of other countries is that the import was large even against the high total of immigration. Thus, it became possible to make more and better use of existing resources, and the measure of their utilization was not less important than their availability and amount, especially in a country where they are not abundant. Interchangeability of capital, space, and other media is a decisive factor, the development of an area is palpably dependent on the supply of capital, and immigration and the lending or investment of capital are interdependent.

But capital gravitates naturally to areas rich in resources and it is improbable that in Israel the substitution of capital for space and natural resources would result from a normal process regulated by purely economic conditions and considerations. On the other hand, accumulation and formation of capital in a developing country is too slow to ensure rapid expansion. Moreover, a part of the investment in transfer and settlement of population must be written off. It follows that transplantation to an area where scarcity of resources is to be offset by a plentitude of capital is feasible only if import of capital is the work of extra-economic factors: a large part of the capital must be of public character, for some of it will be lost in the process.

The extent to which the quality of the newcomers themselves will count in absorption of immigration is described by Eugene Staley as follows:

> Large fixed investments are represented in the special skills of the expert shoemaker, the designer of women's fashions, the mining engineer, the industrial chemist, the expert farmer, the marine navigator, the bone surgeon, the maker of optical goods, the jewel cutter, the horticulturist, the architect of bridges, the irrigation engineer. . . . Finally, there is a human resource not entirely bound to any particular persons but socially carried, and institutionally preserved and fostered: knowledge, especially the sytematic knowledge of science, and industrial techniques based upon it. This resource exists in libraries, in laboratories and universities and public school systems, in the practices of offices and shop and mill, in the traditions of science and the scientific spirit.
>
> Important parts of it are in the "atmosphere" of a particular culture. Knowledge of different kinds and techniques of different kinds are unevenly distributed over the earth today and probably always will be, despite rapid communication, because knowledge is highly specialized. [11]

Transplantation to Israel had the advantage of a proportion of skilled and trained individuals that sufficed to provide its qualitative background. Its composition was well adapted to a shift to secondary and tertiary stages of production and a transformation of Isreal's economy in that direction. The enterprising talents of the population also seemed to fit the task. The traditional Jewish mobility and versatility may well have speeded adaptation.

It is very pertinent that many of the immigrants came from underdeveloped countries of Asia and Africa and their merging with the more sophisticated immigrants from Europe and America was gradual, at times painful, never easy. On the whole, this amalgam of communities was successful and overall levels of productivity were raised considerably; this process was accelerated by the extension of training facilities and education and the cohesive pressures of security and other concerns.

Immigration impelled by extra-economic forces is an outstandingly fruitful source of a population of reasonably diversified occupational cross-section and high output. Indeed, with the exception of Greece, in no other country was transplantation the result of "pushing" forces to such an extent as in Israel. It was entirely on the lines of the early migratory movements, such as the wanderings of Huguenots and Puritans, an edoxus from religious and political opression. This fact and the existence of an economy of growing population were the most distinctive features of the transplantation to Israel.

In most cases, the theory of economic absorption and integration of immigrants puts a great deal of emphasis on conditions in the country of absorption in relation to the size and character of the immigration. Too little attention has been paid hitherto to the fact that immigration itself generated new conditions for its own absorption, or to the dynamic response of the economic structure of the country of immigration, which very process releases new economic forces. Already in Palestine, the Commissioner for Migration had defined that role of immigration:

> Such consequences of themselves lead to a better adaptation of resources and means; and, up to a certain limit, known as the optimum, an increasing population creates new sources of productive activity to meet the needs of the growing people. [12]

The transformation of an economy from subsistance into an exchange economy, and a better utilization of resources, enlarge its absorptive capacity as reflected in Palestine and later in Israel. Expansion, rise, or decline in a process of this type, is due principally to changes in its components and their quantitative nexus. It is all a matter of approximation to an equilibrium of factors making for growth.

This experiment offers evidence that methods of economic expansion may rectify some inner contradictions of modern economy. Even if the conception of an optimum population related to natural resources is accepted, it can be concluded that even deviation from such an optimum would not preclude a rise in the standard of living and full employment if it coincided with a dynamic economic equilibrium established by the impulse that transplantation imparts.

NOTES

1. League of Nations, World Economic Survey, 1938-9 (Geneva), p. 115.

2. Institute of Pacific Relations, The Peopling of Australia, Series No. 4 (Melbourne: Melbourne University Press, 1933), p. 116.

3. W. K. Hancock, Survey of British Commonwealth Affairs, Vol. II, Part, I, (London: Humphrey Milford for Royal Institute of International Affairs, 1940), p. 135.

4. Report to the Secretary of State for Dominion Affairs of the Inter-Departmental Committee on Migration Policy, presented to Parliament, August 1934 (London; H. M. Stationery Office, 1937), pp. 15-17.

5. George H. T. Kimble, The World's Open Spaces (London: Thomas Nelson and Sons, Ltd., 1939), p. 150.

6. Fergus Chalmers Wright, Population and Peace (Paris: International Institute of Intellectual Cooperation, League of Nations, 1939), p. 291.

7. Harold Butler, Problems of Industry in the East, with Special Reference to India, Ceylon, Malaya and the Netherlands Indies (Geneva; International Labour Office, 1938), p. 64.

8. Paul Mombert, "Wirtschaft and Bevölkerung," in Grundriss der Sozialökonomik, II (Tübingen; Verlag I. C. B. Mohr, 1914), pp. 68-69.

9. Sir John Hope Simpson, The Refugee Problem: Report of a Survey (London: Oxford University Press for Royal Institute of International Affairs, 1939), pp. 20-21.

10. G. H. L. F. Pitt Rivers, Problems of Population (London: George Allen and Unwin Ltd., 1932), p. 208.

11. Eugene Staley, World Economy in Transition (New York: Council on Foreign Relations, 1939), p. 73.

12. Government of Palestine, Census of Palestine 1931, Vol. I, Part 1, p. 129.

DEMOGRAPHY

The rapid economic growth of Israel in the period 1948-70 was due, to a very great extent, to a continuous demographic expansion at the exceptionally high annual rate of 5.9 percent (and in the first years of the state, 15.1 percent), by far exceeding the annual increment in countries with a high rate of demographic expansion. In fact, the population of Israel more than trebled during this period. It is true that during the War of Independence some hundreds of thousands of Arabs—the actual figure is controversial—left the part of the territory of Palestine that became the new State of Israel, but their share in the economy of Palestine was rather limited.

Demography is the crucial and conclusive determinant of the economic and social development of Israel. A growth of population far outpacing even the tempo of underdeveloped countries expanded the scope and revolutionized the pattern of society and economy. The population grew from 786,000 on May 15, 1948, to 2,957,800 in 1970, a growth of 265 percent, or more than threefold. The main source of growth was immigration, which accounted for 1.2 million, or 52 percent; natural increase accounted for over a million, or 48 percent. The number of immigrants since the establishment of the state is greater than the number who entered during the entire preceding eighty-year period of Jewish settlement in Palestine.

The birth rate among Jews in Israel in 1969 was 25.6 per thousand, as against 15-19 per thousand in developed countries, indicating a fertility in the Jewish sector much higher than in most developed nations today. One reason is the fairly large proportion of Jews originating from Oriental countries where the rate of population growth is high. Another explanation was put forward by A.M. Carr-Saunders

in the Mandatory period, when the distance between the birth rate of
the Jews of Palestine and that of developed countries was no less:

> The Palestinian Jews are co-operating in an endeavour
> which gives them hope and confidence; moreover, their
> aim is to repeople their former home. Those who are
> concerned about the fall of the birthrate . . . may perhaps
> discern a lesson in this fact and conclude that, if the pro-
> duction rate is to become a replacement rate, people must
> be brought deliberately to found families as a contribution
> to a society in whose future they have confidence and in
> whose ideals they find inspiration. [1]

The growth of the Jewish population chiefly by immigration, was
matched by the rapid and prolific natural increase of the Arab population. The non-Jewish population expanded from 167,000 in 1950 to
430,000 in 1970, a remarkable average annual rise of 3.8 percent,
excluding the addition due to the reunification of Jerusalem; this is
among the highest rates of natural increase in the world.

The non-Jewish birth rate of 46.4 per thousand is high and
rising, but that alone does not account for the exceptional natural
increase. The decline of the Arab death rate is even more significant;
here the influence of the high standard of living and the health and
hygiene services of the Jewish sector is conspicuous, indicating an
immense improvement of Arab well-being which the lower mortality—
in particular of infants—now reflects. Indeed, this is the main factor
that caused a reduction of mortality by as much as 33 percent in two
decades in the Arab minority. Improved health was due in large
measure to such expenditious, comparatively easy, and freely acces-
sible measures as preventive medicine, better sanitation and hygiene,
vaccination, widespread use of sulfa drugs and antibiotics, and notably
the wiping out of malaria by drainage of swamps.

Where the death rate declines in slow motion, as a rule there
are simultaneous changes at work in mental, psychological, and
cultural attitudes to lower the birth rate. But where it drops as far
and as fast as in Israel, such changes cannot keep pace; consequently,
the birth rate falls less than does the death rate and the population
rises rapidly. Israel is no exception to the fact that planned birth-
control is subject to cultural and psychological constraints as well
as social and religious constraints and social pressures that are
generally rigid and conservative.

Comparison of Israel with countries whose population rise has
been most rapid is illuminating: India, 2.2 percent annually; Egypt,
2.5 percent; Latin America, 2.3 percent; and Israel, an average of

5. 9 percent over the past two decades, probably one of the highest percentages of demographic increase in the world during that period, mainly as a result of large-scale immigration.

On the face of it, this demographic increase is a factor promoting economic growth by providing the manpower essential for production to expand as well as by broadening the market with effective purchasing power generated by import of capital to absorb the greater flow of commodities offered by an expanded capacity of production. But it could not always eliminate handicaps to economic development for the following reasons: (1) because the inflow of capital could not always be in step with the growth of population and consequent time lags must have meant lack of coordination between immigration and the arrival of the funds required for new investment and (2) because of bottlenecks in skill and know-how attributable to the make-up of the immigration, whose occupational pattern was not exactly adjusted to an emerging economy shaped by events and by the components of invested capital. It is no easy matter to absorb, integrate, and establish a population that more than trebled in twenty-four years.

In addition, immigration proceeds in a series of waves with each new wave more broadly based than the preceding. Inevitably, there has been uneven fluctuation in population growth and concomitant wide swings of the economic pendulum, particularly in the pre-state period and the first years of the state, with resulting difficulties and frictions of readjustment. The impulses behind these undulant motions are not economic. Immigration to Israel is not subject to the interplay of economic forces and conditions alone; it is also determined by racial, political, and national conditions in other countries and by the impact of the Jewish movement of national renascence.

The exodus of population propelled by noneconomic factors, not conforming to the ordinary type of migratory movements set off by local conditions, is nothing new in history. Immigration into Palestine and Israel has not been simply an economic readjustment by shift from areas of heavier to areas of lighter pressure on resources; its dynamo is political and extra-economic. A frequently quoted analysis of immigration into Palestine appears in the 1935 report of the Commissioner of Migration:

> Jewish immigration into Palestine differs from other migration in that it is not solely the response to economic attractions of the country of immigration. No doubt a proportion of Jewish immigration into Palestine does correspond with ordinary migration in this sense; but a proportion of Jewish immigrants comprises those who have no special interest in Palestine but are repelled

from the countries from which they have emigrated. Natural migration is, in effect, the result of the work of the
country of immigration conceived as a suction-pump; immigration into Palestine is the result of the combined action
of Palestine as a suction-pump and the country of emigration
as a force-pump. And it is this fact which gives sufficient
reason for any difference there may be between the char-
acters and attributes of the Jewish immigrant population in
Palestine and those immigrant populations elsewhere; and
for supposing that a theory of migration accounting for the
phenomenon of immigration generally may not account for
the phenomenon of migration into Palestine. 2

The analysis is even more cogent for immigration into Israel,
the "push" being stronger than the "pull" with the extrusive forces predominant. The social, political, and psychological background of the
displaced persons camps in Germany, the economic and social conditions of Jews in Eastern Europe and the Arab lands of Asia and North
Africa, led to the transplantation of entire communities but vocationally
their members did not answer the needs of the country and an occupational reshuffle became imperative: it was necessary to retrain and
readapt most of them to the jobs the country needed. Only later did
immigration bring people endowed with the necessary skills into the
country, and this process of infusion of know-how was reinforced by
education and vocational training.

The contrast is striking. Hundreds of thousands of former
merchants, peddlers, and clerks had to be absorbed into agriculture,
industry, the army, shipping, and so forth. Almost overnight, these
individuals had to be taught to till the soil, turn a lathe, guard a
frontier, sail the seas. Nor was that the only transformation: they
had to be imbued with the civic spirit and tradition, brought to espouse
the social, economic, and political values that were already fashioned
and crystallized in the new nation. Physical transplantation is a one-
time act, social and economic integration a lengthy process. The
first is a logistic task involving transportation and housing; the second
represents the essence and core of Israel's economic and social
reconstruction. Not a few immigrants were accustomed to European
standards of living, and these had to be preserved within the compass
of a poor and still underdeveloped economy. It would have been
unthinkable—for economic, social, and national reasons—to countenance
two standards of living with one for newcomers from the West and
another for newcomers from the East, and everything had to be done
to equalize standards by a leveling-up operation. Last but not least,
men and women from over a hundred different places of origin,
speaking over fifty languages, and sometimes centuries apart in
cultural evolution, had to be welded into a single ethnic and national

entity while a rapidly growing population was pressing hard upon limited resources.

SCARCITY OF NATURAL RESOURCES

Israel's area of some 8,000 square miles, more than half of it desert and only about a third arable, contains few natural resources. Its conventional water resources, actual and potential, are put at 1,650 million cubic meters per annum and about 95 percent are already utilized. (The main potential source had been the Jordan waters, finally diverted in 1964 at a cost of some $120 million.) In an arid country, the scarcity of water sets stern limits to the expansion of farming.

Natural sources of energy are negligible: there is no coal or hydroelectricity and oil output is a negligible proportion of fuel requirements. What electrical energy there is must to be thermo-generated using imported oil.

Of mineral wealth there are great deposits of potash, bromides, and magnesium in the Dead Sea, fairly substantial phosphatic deposits in the Negev, and about 17 million tons of copper ore of poor content (1.5 percent). All of these, with the exception of magnesium, are commercially exploited.

Timber and other natural resources of value are virtually non-existent.

On this narrow and slender substratum, an economic entity in constant growth is being constructed, to sustain a population in parallel expansion.

THE GEOPOLITICAL SITUATION

Israel, with a population of 3 million, is being implacably warred against by neighboring states with a combined population of some 60 million; at its straitest neck, Israel is only 10 miles across; until mid-1967, there was almost no spot in Israel that could not be brought under enemy gunfire from beyond the frontier. These geopolitical conditions are aggravated by their economic implications: the principle that being comes before well-being makes for a heavy burden of armaments and the wars of 1948, 1956, and 1967 have left their somber imprint on Israel's economy.

Moreover, because of the geopolitical conditions, Israel is deprived of the advantages of its very favorable geographical placement as a link between three continents. Its trade is boycotted by the Arab countries; the Suez Canal is barred to its ships; and land communications with all neighboring states were severed until, after the Six-Day War, the situation was radically modified by what is known as the open-bridges policy which permits and encourages trade between the administered areas and the Arab states despite the unsettled political situation.

Israel's sustained economic growth is reflected in the annual rise of the GNP by 10.6 percent in real terms over the years 1950-70; the corresponding average is 5.5 percent in the European Economic Community, 3 percent in the European Free Trade Area, 3.3 percent in the United States, and 5.0 percent in the underdeveloped countries. Table 4 illustrates this development.

THE TRANSFORMATION OF AGRICULTURE

The transformation of agriculture and the process of industrialization are the main elements of the economic growth of Israel. A greater output of local farming, which is among the vital agents of any such growth, furnished the swiftly multiplying population with an ample supply of foodstuffs: by 1950, local farming was meeting up to 50 percent of the needs of approximately one million consumers; in 1970, it met over 85 percent of the needs of 3 million and on a much higher standard of nutrition.

The objectives of Israel's agricultural policy, dually aimed at ensuring self-sufficiency and at augmenting exports, could be achieved in the main by replacing less valuable by more valuable crops. The smallness of the available area of farmland limited the yield of such energy-producing foodstuffs as cereals and made it imperative to concentrate on such protective ones as dairy products, fruit, and vegetables and on such industrial crops as cotton and groundnuts. Natural conditions ruled out extensive farming as the principal mode of expansion and the emphasis had to be on intensive irrigated agriculture. In an arid country, irrigation is likely to determine the pace and scope of agricultural development. In Israel, an irrigated acre can produce crops paying four to five times more than an unirrigated acre and, under that prompting, in twenty years the area of irrigated land has gone up by 460 percent.

This shift to production of the more profitable protective foodstuffs in the initial period, in the main for the home market, was made possible by a general rise in the standard of living, which

TABLE 4

Net Domestic Product and National Income at Factor Cost,
by Economic Branch, 1952, 1960, and 1969
(IL million)

	1952	1960	1969	Change in Percentages 1952-60	1952-69
Agriculture, forestry, and Fishing	97	410	990	322	920
Industry and mining	184	845	3,412	359	1,754
Construction and public utilities	92	332	1,342	260	1,359
Transport and communication	63	281	1,166	346	1,750
Finance, insurance, and real estate	21	133	792	533	3,671
Ownership of dwellings	44	208	852	372	1,836
Government and non-profit institutions	154	665	2,587	332	1,580
Trade and services	192	656	1,284	241	569
Net domestic product at factor cost	847	3,530	13,481	316	1,491
National income	915	3,626	12,984	296	1,319

Source: Central Bureau of Statistics, Statistical Abstract of Israel, 1970, No. 21. pp. 154-55.

invariably results in a diversion from consumption of energy-producing
to consumption of protective foodstuffs; by extended irrigation and
more investment per agricultural unit of production; and by changing
nutritional habits.

At the same time, agricultural exports, which suffered a setback
during World War II, rose from $6.5 million in 1949 to $140 million
in 1970. Citrus fruits make up the bulk of these exports; the special
economic significance of citriculture is the large capital investment
per earner and the progressive substitution of capital for space, which
means a great deal to a small country with a high population density.
Other agricultural exports also went well forward, particularly in
recent years. For the most part, these include off-season vegetables
and fruit with climatic and soil differences between the exporting and
importing country put to good account; in the circumstances, Europe
is virtually the exclusive market. With improved means of transport,
this is a promising line of development thanks to the steady rise in
consumption of off-season agricultural products that has followed the
remarkable rise in European national incomes.

Better productivity disengages the volume of farm output from
a too-tight dependence on cultivable area. The following specific
examples in Israel illustrate a general trend: the yield of wheat rose
from about 300 kilograms per acre in the 1940's to 740 kilograms in
1969; the annual yield of milk per cow in Israel is 4,890 liters while
in the Netherlands 4,150, in West Germany 3,300, in France 2,225,
in Britain 2,830, and in Greece 800.

In most such comparisons, the extremes of low and high yields
per farmer or unit of production cannot be explained by natural conditions. Interchangeability of artifice and nature seems to have a
major share. An altered pattern of consumption is one such manifes-
tation: lower per capita consumption of carbohydrates and a larger
intake of proteins, correlated with a larger per capita national income,
are to the point.

A highly intensive, irrigated agriculture with selected seeds
and better rotation of crops is very dependent for its development on
large capital investment and much extraneous input of, for example,
fertilizers, machinery, and spare parts, and certain provender for
livestock. But expansion of agriculture is a target of Israel's policy
for reasons that go beyond strict economics, namely, population
dispersal, establishment of a broad rural infrastructure, and diversification of the economy. There is an internal contradiction here:
modern intensive farming needs a large urban market, and natural
conditions and assurance of the farmer's standard of living predicate
it in Israel, but it does reduce the ratio of rural community to total
population.

Writing of Palestine before World War II, Lord Boyd-Orr commented as follows:

> In the Jewish settlement in Palestine, agriculture has been
> raised to such a high level of efficiency that although the
> settlement only occupies 7 percent of the total land, it is
> claimed that it produces about 50 percent of the total agri-
> cultural output. To enable it to reach the high level of
> efficiency, however, there are three workers in other
> industries for one in agriculture.

Contemporary world conditions are very relevant. In the 1960's, food production in the underdeveloped world fell behind demand for reasons set out in an Organization for Economic Cooperation and Development (OECD) study:

> The 1960's has been called a Decade of Development. . . .
> It is therefore a matter for concern that in the first seven
> years of this decade the following phenomena have coincided;
> 1. food production in the developing countries, taken to-
> gether, has grown more slowly than demand,
> 2. the area of good new land that could easily be brought
> under cultivation in developing countries has been sharply
> reduced,
> 3. the population of developing countries has been growing
> at an increasing rate,
> 4. the surplus stocks of grain in North America have
> roughly speaking been exhausted mainly through exports to
> less developed areas,
> 5. development aid from the richer countries has on the
> whole not increased, and
> 6. the debt burden of many developing countries has been
> rising fast. [3]

Demographic, economic, and agrotechnical factors thus complicate the problems of food supply. One problem is the repercussion of large imports of foodstuffs on the balance of payments and the foreign exchange standing of underdeveloped countries.

If diversifying their economies is a sine qua non for the progress and prosperity of the developing countries, then a higher agricultural productivity is the first step toward this goal. The transformation is proceeding in an environment where farm techniques and conditions are rapidly changing out of all recognition. Agriculture, more dependent on nature than any other sector of the economy, is heading toward a major emancipation from natural restraints. By its very essence, it is bound to certain topographical, climatic, and other elements. It is rooted in the soil. But the limits set by nature are

so elastic, so susceptible of continuous expansion, that the full range
of possibilities is still far from being exhausted. If agrarian production
and a country's carrying capacity are conceived as made up of soil,
climate, capital, scope of markets, the farmer's skill, and so forth,
then the effect of topography, climate, and the rest of nature's boons
or banes may be regarded as diminishing in comparison with the man-
made effects of capital, skill, technique, proximity of markets, and
the like. Interchangeability of natural and artificial factors is spreading
quite swiftly.

What could Israel offer toward the solution of this critical, grave,
and peril-ridden problem? It could hardly be a meaningful addition
to the world's food supply: the country is too small for that, its land
and water too scanty. True, its agricultural exports already surpass
$140 million a year and its own production satisfies 85 percent of its
requirements, but measured globally this would be insignificant.

What is important is Israel's role as a laboratory for more
efficient production, for revolutionary methodological changes, and
for the projection of the new methods on the economies of the underdeveloped countries. A study by the Economic Research Service of
the U. S. Department of Agriculture shows that among nineteen countries Israel was first in value of agricultural output per farm worker
and in annual rate of rise, one of the two lowest in illiteracy, the
lowest in infant mortality, and highly ranked in terms of educational
and health levels. The study states:

> Israel, for example, has substantial increases in area of
> crops, in variable and fixed capital per hectare of arable
> land, in level of applied technology, and in the size of its
> agricultural labor force. [4]

This statement is corroborated by the compilation of indexes of total
agricultural production per capita for the year 1968 published by the
Food and Agricultural Organization (FAO) and shown in Table 5.

Between 1950 and 1970, Israel's agricultural production rose
by more than 650 percent and per capita production trebled. The
irrigated area was expanded nearly fivefold. Herds of milk cows
were enlarged almost 3. 2 times, the number of tractors 6 times.
New crops and new tillage were introduced; notable advances were
made in the yield of livestock. Since World War II, exports of citrus
fruit have trebled while the area of groves rose correspondingly and
slightly more. To some extent, the overall rapidity of growth does
reflect a low point of departure, but growth was sustained throughout,
even if at reduced speed toward the end of the period. Productive
capacity expanded in parallel fashion. Gross capital stock in

TABLE 5

FAO Country Index Numbers of Per Capita Total Agricultural Production, 1968
(1952-56 = 100)

Region and Country	1968	Region and Country	1968	Region and Country	1968
Europe		**Latin America**		**Far East (con't.)**	
Austria	139	Argentina	92	Japan	141
Belgium-Luxembourg	120	Bolivia	126	Korea, Rep. of	116
Denmark	115	Brazil	107	Malaysia, West Malaysia	116
Finland	128	Chile	94		
France	134	Colombia	97	Pakistan	100
Germany, Fed. Rep.	124	Costa Rica	121	Philippines	103
Greece	143	Cuba	79	Thailand	120
Ireland	139	Dominican Rep.	75		
Italy	121	Ecuador	134	**African and**	
Netherlands	117	Guatemala	131	**Near East**	
Norway	103	Honduras	115	Afghanistan	107
Portugal	111	Mexico	122	Algeria	71
Spain	133	Panama	112	Cyprus	172
Sweden	101	Paraguay	95	Ethiopia	115
Switzerland	105	Peru	95	Iran	118
United Kingdom	132	Uruguay	84	Iraq	107
Yugoslavia	151	Venezuela	129	Israel	192
				Libya	118
North America		**Far East**		Morocco	115
Canada	99	Burma	107	South Africa	114
United States	102	Ceylon	108	Sudan	116
		China, Taiwan	112	Syria	95
Oceania		India	100	Tunisia	90
Australia	127	Indonesia	94	Turkey	115
New Zealand	119			United Arab Rep.	106

Note: Figures represent per capita production in terms of each country's total population.

Source: FAO, Production Yearbook, Vol. 23 (1969).

agriculture rose by 228. 5 percent, and the number of gainfully employed was 24. 6 percent higher in 1970 than in 1952 (see Table 6).

The inputs of labor and capital were practically constant in the
period 1962-69, but higher productivity offset this. The principal
instruments of change were the skills empirically mastered by the
newly settled farmers, a penetrating extension service of professional
instructors, and research. Typical examples are shown in Table 7.
This progress made it possible to maintain the rise in income per
employed person, which was about 257 percent (calculated at constant
consumer prices) between 1952 and 1969.

Thus, an export-minded, highly mechanized, computer-guided
and planned agriculture is seen to display an impressive gamut of
prospects for stepping up productivity if the requisite inputs of capital
and skill can be counted on. With modern technology, there is no
doubt that farm production can be quickly even spectacularly enlarged.
Israel's experience is of particular interest because the successes
were won by a population that was overwhelmingly untutored in agriculture and had to undergo an occupational reshuffle in an arid country
with few natural resources and little water. Success was achieved
principally by applying capital, know-how, and science. The value of
production per employed person rose in real terms by over 238 percent
from 1955 to 1970 and its average is now ten times higher than in
developing countries as well as higher than in France, West Germany,
or Japan. On one million acres with only 10. 5 percent of the population
engaged in farming, foodstuffs are produced for 85 percent of nearly
three million consumers and, on top of that, nutritional standards
were improved considerably and farm produce worth $140 million is
shipped or flown to overseas markets. In some branches, such as
milk and cotton, Israel can claim the highest unit yield in the world.

If the developing countries were to expand their farm output by
1985 at the annual rate of Israel, the predictable gap between rising
demand for foodstuffs and their supply could be bridged and the standard
of nutrition considerably raised.

In the course of time, Israel's agriculture became more diversified and export-oriented (see Table 8). Apart from citrus, exports
of off-season fruit, flowers, and vegetables to European markets
shot up by leaps and bounds.

Yet although the population grew, nutrition improved, and exports
of farm produce expanded, between 1955 and 1970 the proportion of
farmers in Israel's total manpower fell from 17. 6 percent to 10. 5
percent and the value of their output in the GNP fell from 11. 8 percent
to 9 percent. Furthermore, the pace of annual growth of output slowed

TABLE 6

Key Indicators of Economic Growth, 1952, 1960, and 1970

Total	1952	1960	1970	Percentage Increase
Capital stock (million dollars at 1966 prices)	305.8	653.2	1,004.5	228.5
Gainfully employed (thousands)	85.0	119.4	105.9	24.6
Gross product (million dollars at 1967 prices)	128.3	302.1	551.2	329.6
Per employed Capital stock (dollars)	3,598	5,471	9,485	163.6
Gross product (dollars)	1,509	2,530	5,205	244.9

Source: Research Department, Bank of Israel.

TABLE 7

Change in Average Yields of Selected Crops, 1955-69

Crop	Percentage Change
Wheat (per unit of land)	106
Barley	69
Sorghum for grain, irrigated	247
Cotton lint, irrigated	38
Milk (per cow)	6

Source: Central Bureau of Statistics, Statistical Abstract of Israel, 1955-69.

TABLE 8

Exports of Agricultural Products, 1960-70
(million dollars)

Year	Value	Year	Value
1960	37.8	1966	62.0
1961	52.6	1967	88.5
1962	59.8	1968	87.2
1963	39.1	1969	114.4
1964	40.8	1970	140.2
1965	61.8		

in the late 1960's to 3-4 percent, mainly because of the saturation of the home market; export orientation in produce other than citrus, although expanding, is still only beginning. The scarcity of water is also a limiting factor. The consequence is that industry is now the chief source of any rise in the GNP.

The experiment in economic growth in Israel started with a clean slate and was unencumbered by inherited and continuous tradition or by any crystallized and frozen forms and methods. The spirit of innovation and bold venturing ruled not only in the kaleidoscope of a socioeconomic polymorphia, with the attendant advantages of flexibility in multiplying and diversifying and, therefore, of an interadaptability of economic organisms, but also in technology, with none of the fetters of archaic and antiquated ways handed down uncritically from generation to generation. This departure was particularly noticeable in farming where, in most branches, new methods and new technology in irrigation, rotation of crops, and use of fertilizers led to record crops and yields. As noted, in the beginning, expansion of urban markets, the growing experience of new settlers, and technological inventiveness helped and hastened this rural revolution.

The exploration of novel and unorthodox avenues of approach in economic organization, in social forms of enterprise, and in technology was not without its many failures and sometimes waste of resources, but in the last resort it proved rewarding, blazing trails and speeding up economic growth, with agriculture a main beneficiary. Jewish farming began by copying the primitive Arab farming which was characterized by wooden ploughs and draught animals and focused mainly on cultivation of cereals, but this brief competition with Arab husbandry and its cheap labor was hopeless. Subsequent attempts to develop viticulture for making wine failed as well and many vineyards had to be uprooted. Citriculture responded more profitably and lastingly and soon became a main export branch. Subsequently, mixed farming applied itself strenuously both to supplying a domestic urban market that welcomed its dairy produce and poultry and to growing fruits and vegetables, in part for shipping to European centers in the off-season.

Systematized agricultural research and training help to intensify and amplify the steady qualitative and quantitative development of Israel's agriculture. Liberal allocations for research, a network of experimental stations, diffusion of the results of research and trial through a widespread extension service and teams of instructors—all these have been factors in perfecting and realizing the plans of agricultural expansion and in bringing about the changeover to a new and multistructured mosaic with higher quantitative and qualitative levels of production. The use of technical and managerial achievements and of modern equipment, also played key roles in this process.

To sum up, the technical progress and exploits of Israel's farming today can be explained by the lack of rigid tradition and obsolete methods; the need to evolve new branches of production in lieu of vain competition with an obsolescent and unremunerative economy; the intelligence, flexibility, and dynamism of the human potential; propitious climatic conditions and proximity to many urban shoppers in Europe and at home; and, perhaps first and foremost, the will and readiness to experiment, to adopt new technologies, to switch from one line of yield to another, and to acquire and apply scientific methods and new technologies.

INDUSTRIALIZATION

This development led to greater urbanization, a trend encouraged by rapidly expanding industry. A good indicator of industrial growth is the number of workers employed, which was 247,000 in 1969 as opposed to only 89,000 in 1950. Output rose more quickly than numbers because of higher productivity, greater mechanization, and the use of labor-saving devices.

Since factory production is made up of many diverse elements, the most conclusive pointers of its growth would be those connected with the value of output (always provided that price fluctuations are eliminated), utilization of electric power in physical terms, and the payroll. Table 9 provides an intertemporal comparison on that tripartite basis.

A set of explanatory circumstances peculiar to Israel must be sought. The motives of industrialization that are frequently met in a developing country are lacking in Israel. It is not a country that has been a source of raw materials for many years. Cheap labor and those materials close at hand eventually attract capital from developed countries and new industries strike root. With such a process, immigration has little if any link: a sprinkling of experts and skilled workers is all that is necessary to get the plants going and the finance is imported. Israel does not enjoy these incentives: there is no cheap labor and raw materials are very scarce.

Not infrequently, industrialization may be ascribed to a shift of labor and resources from primary to secondary production leading to a better equilibrium, a more balanced and diversified economy, higher standards of living, and fuller employment. Industrialization based on transplantation of population takes on a different character: more inhabitants and a consequent extension of markets support it. Without concomitant industrialization in the country of immigration, transplantations are not likely to work. Agriculture by itself cannot

TABLE 9

Indicators of Growth in Factory Production,
1950, 1960, and 1969

	1950	1960	1969
Output (IL million, 1966 prices)	1,450	3,660	10,031
Exports ($ million)	18	146	554
Of which: Diamonds	9	56	216
Employed (thousands)	89	162	247
Electricity consumption (kwh million)	141	669	1,715

absorb a large increment of population within a short space of time, and its transformation is almost inconceivable without expanding urban markets. But industrialization can be accomplished by the very process of transplantation if that process is allied with import of investment capital, the entry of experts and skilled labor, and the enlarged markets that immigration itself produces.

Decentralization and a far-reaching freedom from subservience to local raw materials and natural conditions are the marks of the world's industrial development in the postwar era. In the past, industry inclined to concentrate in especially favored areas: "The existence of a large market and of transport, banking and commercial facilities, as well as the convenience of proximity to related and subsidiary forms of production, abundant supplies of skilled labor and technical knowledge, and saving of time and interest charges"[5] were the advantages that drew new industry to regions where large-scale industrial organization already existed. However, technical progress tends to undermine established positions. Modern simplified processes are easily learned by new countries and the ever-changing emphasis of demand lends an impetus to the establishment of new industries in new places. The development of transport, and a wider margin of costs between price of raw materials and price of finished product, made this quicker and added to the importance of such politicoeconomic factors as the availability of capital, tariffs, supply of skilled labor, and marketing facilities in determining where this or that industry should be set up.

The spread of the industrial revolution is described and explained as follows:

> A second factor which has an important bearing on the
> location of industry is the cost of transportation. . . .
> Transport costs, and especially sea freights, being lower,
> are a less important factor in the localization of indus-
> tries, which are therefore attracted by other forces such
> as increasing consumers' demand.[6]

Thus, industry is no longer localized in a few favored spots. The
highest gains in industrial output in our time were in agrarian and
not industrial states, which is indicative of the wide geographical
diffusion of industry. G. G. Smith writes:

> Scientific progress and technological invention which used
> to lend support to a free trade policy are now among the
> most powerful of forces encouraging economic nationalism.
> Standardization of processes and output, development of
> intricate machine tools which can be operated by compar-
> atively unskilled labor after a brief period of training,
> wide distribution of electrical power and the growth of
> technical education in every branch of industry, enable
> new factories to be set up with equal prospects of success
> almost anywhere throughout the world. So Lancashire
> finds competitors in India and Japan; and Irish Free State
> workers come to the Midlands for a few months' training
> and return home to operate factories for holloware, gloves,
> hosiery, and many other commodities in little centres
> selected at random which never before had an industry of
> any kind.[7]

Consequently, industry is concentrating more and more in areas
unendowed with generous stocks of own raw materials. Despite their
lack of any important raw materials, Belgium, which "is almost
completely dependent on imported raw materials,"[8] has the highest
proportion of population engaged in manufacturing, namely, 47.8 percent, with Switzerland second with 44.9 percent.[9] Thus, in industry
a country's own natural resources are becoming interchangeable with
captial, skill, and knowledge, which depend on educational level and
occupational structure, and with deliberate policies of industrialization.[10]

A cardinal condition of industrial expansion is an economy of
growing population. The conclusion is that "an increase in working
population is injurious to economic welfare in a predominantly primary
producing country, beneficial to economic welfare in a predominantly
industrial country, and that the ill-effects of the former can be mitigated by a rapid transfer of population away from primary production.[11]

Thus, the Malthusian theory is reversed in countries undergoing transition from predominantly primary to secondary and tertiary stages of production.[12] This bears significantly on the problem of the capacity of countries that are in the process of industrialization to absorb new population. The Malthusian theory no longer applies to them since industry represents a net accession of wealth and production unrelated to space or natural resources.

An economy of growing population is correlated with industrial development, first by providing more markets and second because expanding markets reduce industrial costs and raise industrial productivity in three ways:

1. A certain minimum demand is necessary for transition from handicraft to factory. A correlation between the size of enterprises and high productivity is manifest in periods of transition since industry depends on the extent of marketing facilities.

2. As industry as a whole expands, greater specialization and subdivision, with resulting economies in production, are possible. Such auxiliary industries as repair workshops finishing and dyeing plants in textiles can be established. Allyn Young propounds the theory that industrial growth is correlated with the size of industry as a whole and not, as is usually assumed, with the size of individual plants. Thus, high productivity per worker is dependent on the relative growth of industry as a whole. This seems to be the fruition of increasing specialization among the factories.[13]

3. More and easier marketing facilitates a higher degree of utilization of existing plant and labor, a very influential factor in determining the cost of production.

Thus, an expanding population enhances industrial productivity and reduces the costs of industrial production. At the same time, by establishing technical and economic minima of production, it makes possible the production of a wider variety of industrial goods. This goes far to explain the inapplicability of Malthusian doctrines to economic growth in countries that are undergoing industrialization and for example: "there is no proof that the industrialized countries of Western Europe are overpopulated."[14] Since most of Israel's industry produces for the home market, it is orientated toward a growing population and its expanding demand. Thus, as has been seen, industrialization is made possible by transplantation itself, linked with import of capital for investment in industry, entry of experts and skilled labor, and the expanding markets that immigration opens. Industry's global tendency toward decentralization and its release in such large measure from dependence on what nature provides faster development in a country like Israel, with few natural resources, now that local natural resources are becoming increasingly inter-changeable with other factors of production.

Moreover, the policy of protecting infant industry was applied in somewhat extreme form in Israel, and markedly at the very beginning: tariffs were prohibitive in some cases or imports of competing products were administratively restricted, which meant that a number of inefficient plants came into existence. But the policy was gradually reversed towards the end of the second decade. The reversal of certain policies and the saturation of the home market, as well as the arrival of a new category of experts and entrepreneurs, induced a structural change that is clearly brought out in Table 10.

The relative decline of such staple manufactures as food and textiles and the growth of such more sophisticated products as machinery and electrical and electronic equipment unmistakably reflect a structural change in Israel's industry. However, in the long run any further expansion depends, in constantly larger measure, on the ability of industrial exports to make their way into foreign markets and on a growth of such exports; with its spatial and natural limitations, Israel has no option but to obtain the wherewithal of its production by stepping up exports.

Industry, to start with, is powerfully attracted to markets, which become a decisive factor in determining its location; thus, the most potent consideration in industrial expansion is an economy of growing population. Israel takes advantage of this. The economy of growing population, as explained, is part and parcel of industrial development: it provides bigger and better markets and keeps expanding them, and in due course larger-scale production reduces costs and raises productivity. In addition, given enough purchasing power, a growing population makes it possible, by establishing technical and economic minima of production, to turn out an ever wider range of products.

In the course of time, industry, under structural modification, became more export-oriented. Israel's industrial exports rose from $23 million in 1949 to $595 million in 1970 and are expected to reach $700 million in 1971, an increase of 17.6 percent over the preceding year, while the share of exports in total industrial production rose from less than 10 percent in 1949 to 25 percent in 1969 and 1970.

The placement of many plants is in constantly greater measure determined by such factors as an industrial milieu, which comprises more than just availability of skilled labor and depends on science and know-how, research laboratories and training schools, tradition, managerial ability, and techniques.

TABLE 10

Net Output of Industry by Main Branches,
1950, 1960, and 1970

	1950	1960	1970
Mines and quarries	2.4	1.7	2.0
Food	26.3	20.2	19.7
Textiles and clothing	22.5	18.9	14.1
Wood and wood products	8.2	6.8	6.0
Paper and printing	3.3	5.6	4.0
Leather and leather products	2.8	3.4	2.4
Rubber and plastics	1.4	2.7	3.2
Chemicals and oil refining	6.1	10.6	8.8
Nonmetallic minerals	6.1	4.7	3.5
Diamonds	2.2	4.6	6.9
Metals, total	16.7	19.1	27.8
Of which: Basic metals	n.a.	2.4	2.8
Metal products	n.a.	6.7	5.0
Machinery	n.a.	2.8	6.0
Electrical and electronic equipment	n.a.	2.9	6.0
Transportation equipment	n.a.	4.3	8.0
Miscellaneous industries	2.0	1.7	1.6
Total	100.0	100.0	100.0

   More than once, immigration has been the harbinger of industrial
growth. Huguenot refugees from France in Reformation days and
Puritans arriving in an embryo America brought their crafts with
them. The wool industry was developed in England by Flemish
emigrés, the clothing industry in the United States by Russian Jewish
newcomers in the 1890's. It is natural for artisans and other such
workers to seek to ply their familiar trades in the new environment,

which is a powerful factor in reproducing in a young country the manufactures of its immigrants' more advanced industrial origins.

Development in Israel, which made full use of this trend, proceeded in two main directions—the lists are illustrative, not exhaustive:

1. Development of industries based on local raw materials,
such as the production of fertilizers out of the huge mineral deposits
of the Dead Sea, with the accent on potash and bromides; phosphatic
deposits in the Negev; copper mining on a modest scale near Eilat on
the Red Sea; the processing into foodstuffs of such farm produce as
citrus, fruits, and vegetables; the kilning of cement and the making
of other building materials; and textile spinning and weaving from
locally grown cotton.

2. Development of industries manufacturing imported raw
materials, for which skill and know-how constitute Israel's only relative advantage. Such manufacturing is possible because either the
stuff involved is very light (diamonds for instance) so that the freight
differential is negligible or the materials represent no more than a
fraction of the value of the finished product, as with some kinds of
machinery and instruments, and in electronics. Israel has the advantages of reasonably plentiful skilled labor and entrepreneurial initiative, a high scientific potential, a fairly low level of wages for skilled
labor and trained management, and an abundance of professional and
technical knowledge.

The very circumstance that immigration into Israel was, to no
negligible extent, the effect of extra-economic causes raised the
percentage of skills, training, and expertise in the totality of arrivals.
That is to say, Israel's industrialization is the result of a linkage—
by immigration—of capital import and population growth, in other
words, of transplantation in its three aspects:

1. An expanding population provided a sufficiently large home
market and, by establishing technical and economic minima and
cheapening production, opened up possibilities for diversified industry,
particularly under conditions of far-reaching tariff protection and
administrative measures in the initial period of development.

2. Skilled labor, initiative, and specialized knowledge were
opportunely introduced.

3. Capital imports were linked with immigration.

With the evolving of a modern economy, the tertiary stage of
production, including state services, expanded absolutely and

relatively, corresponding to a rise in national income. By reason of higher output per worker, which rose by 5.3 percent per year in the overall economy between 1950 and 1970, the improvement in all principal lines of production outstripped the growth of population. The advantages of larger-scale production and greater capital investment, with concurrent improvement and extension of capital equipment and vocational training, contributed to the rise in productivity and thus to sustained economic growth.

CONSTRUCTION

Building has acted as a channel through which purchasing power is pumped into economic life and effective demand stimulated. This has been accomplished not by organized planning but, again, by an extraneous factor: the influx of capital and immigrants. The newcomers signify a continuous requirement of housing, and that requirement is fulfilled by new construction underwritten by the capital influx. An exceptionally high proportion of investment in building goes to wages, creating a market for the products of farm and factory. In that way, the demand for consumer goods has kept ahead of supply and the new capital sunk in building could thus bear indirectly and immediately on the economy, always provided that the inflationary impact of such a process can be neutralized by a sufficient inflow of capital, which would finance the ensuing excess of imports over exports and thus counteract its detrimental effects on the balance of payments. There was never enough housing for a multiplying population and, as each wave of immigration broke on its shores and its economy went forward, provision of homes was Israel's chief preoccupation.

At first, all of Israel's economy fluctuated with the ups and downs of building, which has become as sensitive a barometer of business conditions as iron and steel output elsewhere. The extent of fluctuation may be seen in the undulant graph of building and the correspondence between building and such other economic indicators as imports and government revenue.

Building lays down a stratum of local consumers and relies on a cumulative demand reinforced by steady large-scale immigration. Thus, in the beginning the country's expansion was based on an industry that, because of the immigration, encountered no marketing problem and made possible a subsequent shift to production for the home buyer. Ongoing immigration, along with an inflow of capital, brings with it an equally constant and valuable increment of purchasing power: it provides just that much sought "external consumer" who is independent of the normal circle of the economy within which a disproportion arises between production and purchasing power.

Thus, heavy investment in building, about $5,320 million at pegged prices since 1950, was a response to mass immigration progressively in need of more and better housing, and also was a stimulus to general industrial development. The share of building workers in the total labor force was very large: there was a peak of 10.5 percent in 1965, dropping to 8.9 percent in 1969, but the drop was appreciably offset by an injection of modern technology. The data exhibit the preponderant weight of the investment sector in the economy of Israel.

NOTES

1. A. M. Carr-Saunders, World Population, Past Growth and Present Trends (Oxford: Clarendon Press for Royal Institute for International Affairs, 1936), p. 22.

2. Government of Palestine, Department of Migration, Annual Report, 1935, p. 26.

3. OECD, The Food Problem of Developing Countries (Paris, 1968), p. 10.

4. U.S. Department of Agriculture, Changes in Agriculture in 26 Developing Nations, 1948 to 1963, Foreign Agricultural Economic Report No. 27 (Washington, D.C.: GPO, November 1965).

5. Leage of Nations, World Economic Survey, 1931-32 (Geneva).

6. Ibid., pp. 18, 19, 20.

7. The Royal Economic Society, Economic Journal (London), December 1935, p. 624.

8. The Economist, May 1, 1943, p. 555.

9. Colin Clark, The Conditions of Economic Progress (London: MacMillan and Co. Ltd., 1940), p. 183.

10. H. Frenkel, "Industrialization of Agricultural Countries and the Possibilities of New International Division of Labor," Economic Journal, June-September 1943, p. 194.

11. Clark, op. cit., p. 154.

12. Ibid., p. 6.

13. Ibid., p. 11.

14. Carr-Saunders, op. cit., pp. 142-43.

3

The Palestine Commissioner for Migration defined the test of the economic utility of Jewish immigration as follows in 1936:

> The test, the only test, of the economic utility of Jewish immigration into Palestine in relation to the absorptive capacity of the country conceived in an economic sense is the variation in real income or standard of life. [1]

During the period under review in this chapter, the decade 1960-71, there was a remarkable rise in private consumption and in the standards of living of all sectors of the population. The most revealing indicators of income are those that reflect personal per capita consumption in real terms, which rose at an average annual rate of 4. 9 percent in the years 1950-71.

In the second decade, 1957/58-1968/69, the standard of living went up notably: real per capita consumption rose by almost 70 percent, which is an average annual rate of 4. 9 percent, while real monetary income per family rose by almost 120 percent, an average annual rate of 7. 4 percent. The ownership of durable goods, specifically of electric appliances and private cars, as shown in Table 11, reflects this trend. Obviously, if 96 percent of families own electric refrigerators and 88 percent own cooking appliances, they can hardly be considered as destitute, although it must be conceded that climatic conditions make refrigerators a vital commodity in Israel. The rapid growth of ownership of television sets, washing machines, and the rest is further confirmation of that inference.

Housing conditions also are an important index of living standards, especially in a country of rapid demographic expansion in

TABLE 11

Growth in Ownership of Electric Appliances and Private Cars

Appliance	Year	Percentage of Families	Year	Percentage of Families
Electric refrigerators	1960	51.0	1970	96.0
Washing machines	1960	17.0	1970	46.0
Hot plates and ranges	1960	64.0	1969	88.0
Mixers	1962	9.2	1970	27.7
Television sets	1965	2.4	1970	53.0
Private cars	1962	4.1	1970	17.0

which it is difficult to keep pace with a constantly increasing demand
for homes. From the beginning of the decade until 1969, the proportion of families with a residential density of three persons per
room or more fell from 21 percent to 9 percent of the total of families,
while the proportion with a residential density of one person or less
per room rose from 7 percent to 16 percent of that total. The lesser
share of food in total consumption expenditure also attests to steadily
improving standards of living (see Table 12).

Government expenditure on social services, health, and education developed from IL 97 million within a total of IL 778 million in
1955-56 to IL 1,303 million within a total of IL 4,328 million in 1965-
66, a rate of growth, far higher than that of the population, even
allowing for price rises. Infant mortality, at 12.6 per thousand, com-
pares favorably with the most progressive states such as New Zealand,
14.0; Sweden, 13.7; Switzerland, 12.0; United States, 12.7; and
Britain, 20.2. Life expectancy at birth is 70.5 years for men and
73.6 for women, as compared with 68 and 73 years, respectively, in
New Zealand; 72 and 75 in Sweden; 66 and 71 in Switzerland; 67 and
74 in the United States, and 68 and 74 in Britain.

Comparative data for health services are as follows: in 1967,
Israel spent 5.9 percent of its GNP on health services, as against
5.6 percent in Chile, 5.5 percent in Canada and the United States,
4.9 percent in Australia, 4.4 percent in Yugoslavia, 4.5 percent in
Finland, and 4.2 percent in France. The number of inhabitants per
doctor in Israel was 422; the comparable figures were 430 in the
U.S.S.R., 650 in the United States, 710 in Denmark, 850 in Sweden,
860 in Britain, 1,230 in Lebanon, and 2,320 in Egypt.

Still, the most comprehensive of all indicators is per capita
national income at constant prices and, even more important, the
dynamic trend of the figures over the years. In Israel, that trend
is unmistakable: taking 1950 as the base year, the figures for per
capita national income for 1965 and 1969 were 250 and 293, respectively. Data on family expenditures likewise point to better standards
of living. Table 13 shows the improvement in real income per family,
price fluctuations aside, in the years 1957/58-1968/69.

Since taxation in Israel is steeply progressive and social welfare
services are rendered mainly to low-income families, the distribution
of real net income is more egalitarian than that of gross income.
Nevertheless, it is evident that the material conditions of some groups
are still unsatisfactory and in particular their housing is substandard.
What is defined in subjective, arbitrary, and social value terms as
the "poverty line" is no different from that of Western Europe. Pockets
of poverty do exist, but they are becoming smaller and fewer as time

TABLE 12

Breakdown of Average Expenditure of Urban Wage-Earner's Family,
Selected Years, 1956/57-1968/69
(percentages)

	1956/57	1959/60	1963/64	1968/69
Total expenditure	100	100	100	100
Food	39	36	31	27
Housing	12	12	14	13
Dwelling and household maintenance	8	8	7	6
Furniture and household equipment	7	8	9	8
Health, education, culture, and entertainment	11	13	14	18
Clothing and footwear	12	11	10	10
Transport, cigarettes, and services	9	10	13	16
Membership dues and gifts	2	2	2	2

TABLE 13

Gross Monetary Income Per Adult, Selected Years, 1957/58-1968/69

Decile group	Real Rate of Increase (percentages)		
	1963/64 Compared with 1957/58	1968/69 Compared with 1963/64	1968/69 Compared with 1957/58
Lowest	63	33	117
Second	57	19	87
Third	49	21	80
Fourth	51	18	78
Fifth	53	19	82
Sixth	49	22	83
Seventh	49	18	84
Eighth	48	26	87
Ninth	49	28	91
Highest	57	24	95
Average	52	24	89

43

goes on and as general economic progress and prosperity have their effect.

The repercussions of the economic process of immigrant absorption on Israel's standard of living, as measured by consumption indexes, strengthen the conclusion, based on production data, that it has been effective and that the standard of living of the population, in terms of general level of consumption and consumpton of typical goods, has risen appreciably. Any average level of per capita income might hide a maldistribution of income and the prevalence of poverty and destitution among groups of the population, but on the whole the distribution of national income in Israel tends toward reasonable standards of equality.

One fact in the world is outstanding, namely, the existence of two groups: (1) the developed and industrialized countries where the gap in standards is narrow and (2) the developing or, rather, underdeveloped, countries, where the gap is very wide. Whatever the criterion, as far as that gap is concerned Israel belongs to the group of developed and industrialized countries. Its standard of living is set in no small part by the remarkably comprehensive social services—education, health, housing—provided by the state and by a wage structure with only slight differentials. Progressive taxation redistributes national income effectively. The government aims to establish a welfare state and to maintain full employment, and all its policies are shaped accordingly.

It is true that technological changes, conducive as they were to a sharper differentiation in wages and salaries, the spells of inflation due to unorthodox financing of large scale immigration and other needs, and the rise in land values have led to an accumulation of wealth by some sections whereby the traditional spirit of egalitarianism has weakened somewhat. Immigrants with a lower level of education and few skills gave momentum to this retrogression in the first decade, and the arrival of skilled and trained professionals from the West in the second decade magnified the disparity. But, as immigrants acquire new skills and are integrated into the economy, the differences narrow. Government policy seeks to level out and rapidly unify the diverse communities and to blend the new into the veteran population. An additional factor intensifying the social disparities and widening the economic gap was the 1965-67 recession, which resulted in large-scale unemployment. Between 1967 and 1971 the trend was reversed and the social and economic gap between groups was narrowed by a government policy of, in particular, progressive taxation, full employment, and general education and training.

The Lorenz curve (see Table 14) marks the resultant degree of equality in income distribution in Israel as being in the range of several

TABLE 14

Coefficient of Inequality in
Gross Income in Israel, 1967-70

| Period | Coefficient | |
	Per Urban Family	Per Wage-Earner
1967	0.416	0.365
1968	0.384	0.339
1969	0.378	0.316
1970	0.375	0.305

of the more egalitarian of developed countries: The inequality coeffi-
cient, based on tax data and on a distribution by decile groups, was
0.354 for the total population of Norway (1963); 0.377 for Denmark
(1963); and 0.388 for Britain (1964). For wage and salary earners,
it was 0.268; for Sweden (1963); 0.395 and 0.357 respectively; for the
Netherlands (1962), 0.427 and 0.390; for West Germany (1964), 0.446
and 0.271; for Finland (1962), 0.460; for France (1962), 0.339 for
wage and salary earners; and for Israel (1960-61), 0.370 for the
whole. There can be no question that Israel is diametrically different
from other developing countries with regard to income distribution.
In Israel, as is shown in Table 15, the share of income in the two
lowest deciles is among the highest and that in the highest decile is
the lowest excepting Norway. To sum up, the distribution of Israel's
national income is characterized by remarkably narrow differentials
thanks to the government's welfare state program, a highly organized
labor movement, progressive taxation, full employment, and the
rapid assimilation of immigrants into the economy. Nevertheless,
it is more differentiated than it was in the 1950's when an extremely
egalitarian tendency ruled and led to far-reaching erosion of significant
and substantial differences. Immigration induced a dual expansion:
a horizontal quantitative broadening of the population base and a
vertical rise in consumption levels.

The voluminous import of capital serves mainly to expand investment, but some of it does augment consumption by enlarging
purchasing power and thus, by its percolation into that channel, raises
the standard of living. Swift economic growth assures full employment and thus generates larger incomes as well as helping to step up
real wages by 4.6 percent annually during the 1960's. Thanks to

TABLE 15

Income Distribution Among Total Population Based on Tax Data, Selected Countries

Decile Group	Great Britain 1964	West Germany 1964	Netherlands 1962	Denmark* 1963	Norway 1963	Sweden 1963	Finland 1962	Israel 1960–61
Lowest	2.0	2.1	1.3	1.7	1.0	1.6	0.5	1.3
Second	3.1	3.2	2.7	3.3	3.5	2.8	1.9	3.6
Third	4.2	4.7	4.2	4.7	5.3	4.1	3.5	5.1
Fourth	6.0	5.4	5.8	6.1	6.8	5.5	5.2	6.8
Fifth	7.5	6.5	7.4	7.7	8.5	7.7	6.8	8.4
Sixth	9.1	7.2	8.6	9.1	10.0	9.7	8.6	9.6
Seventh	11.0	8.4	10.0	10.9	11.3	11.4	11.1	11.1
Eighth	12.9	9.6	11.6	13.3	13.1	13.2	13.1	12.3
Ninth	14.9	11.5	14.6	16.1	15.6	16.1	16.8	16.1
Highest	29.3	41.4	33.8	27.1	24.9	27.9	32.5	25.7
Inequality Coefficient	.388	.446	.427	.377	.354	.395	.460	.370

Note: The statistical unit is the taxpayer.

*Income after tax.

Sources: United Nations, Income in Post-War Europe, (Geneva, 1967); Israel: Committee in Israel appointed by the Prime Minister, Minister of Finance, Governor of the Bank of Israel and Secretary General of the Labor Federation, headed by David Horowitz, Report of the Committee for the Examination of Income Distribution (Jerusalem: Government and Bank of Israel, 1971).

economic growth, the effects of the pressure exerted on limited natural resources by a proliferation of inhabitants were to some extent counteracted and neutralized.

Despite all these indications of equalizing factors and egalitarian tendencies, there was an aggravation of friction, labor unrest, and social ferment in the late 1960's. This occurred despite the country's security situation, which should have led to the tempering of demands for higher incomes and full employment, and despite a remarkable rise in the standard of life during this period. The number of work-days lost by strikes increased from 102,000 in 1969 to 390,000 in 1970. To some extent, these phenomena are a reflection of world-wide tendencies and trends.

The pressure for higher living standards frequently results in a situation where income advances faster than productivity, with a consequent slowdown in economic growth and sometimes a substantial rise in the unemployment rate. These trends are reinforced by the responsiveness of governments and employers to the demands of broad sections of the population for higher incomes and fringe benefits, which is an inherent feature of a democratic regime, as well as by the rigidity of institutional factors. The combination of electoral considerations and the pressure exerted by the trade unions sometimes pushes the income level up beyond what is economically advisable, thereby generating inflationary tendencies.

All these factors operate in Israel on an intensified scale. The more affluent the society—it should be borne in mind that Israel's consumption increased by some 25 percent per capita over the past four years—the more insistent are the demands for still higher living standards. The affluence of a society like Israel's does not necessarily mitigate such social pressures. On the contrary, the demonstration effect of the particularly ostentatious standards of consumption of certain small but conspicuous sectors of the population heightens aspirations and accentuates demands. Overfull employment strengthens the bargaining power of almost every group in the population. Conspicuous and competitive consumption becomes the rule rather than the exception. In an economy of overfull employment inflated by heavy defense spending, it is extremely difficult to implement a policy of restraint.

In Israel, the feeling of dissatisfaction with the income levels attained so far is aggravated by the fact that immigrants from Asia and Africa generally are found in the less skilled categories of labor and also have large families, which further depresses their living standards.

The communal differences, rooted in the origins of the various sectors of the population, are gradually being eliminated or at least reduced by deliberate government policies and the general prosperity in which all sectors of the population are sharing. But in the transition period social and communal friction is leading to clashes and conflicts that, although affecting only a rather limited part of the population, are seriously hampering Israel's ability to reach its goal of economic independence. Paradoxically, overfull employment and more affluence, as well as the narrowing of the inequality gap, do not assuage the feeling of discontent or moderate the demands for higher standards but, rather, exacerbate the clashes and conflicts inherent in these trends and tendencies.

NOTE

1. Government of Palestine, Department of Migration, Annual Report, 1936, p. 28.

CAPITAL AND ECONOMIC GROWTH

If any universal conclusions are to be drawn from the case study of Israel as to the possibilities and pattern of economic growth, that process itself must be analyzed and its components scrutinized. No underdeveloped country can achieve sustained economic growth without capital in quantity:

> When numbers are growing rapidly there is a strong and fairly steady increase in the demand for almost every commodity, for food, for clothes, for housing, for coal, and for almost everything else that satisfies the multifarious wants of human life. To meet this increasing demand, the supply of the various commodities must be correspondingly increased. The labor required for this purpose is, of course, readily available, as a consequence of the growth of numbers. But goods are not produced by means of labor alone, but by labor in cooperation with capital equipment and with natural resources.
>
> Accordingly a condition of rapidly growing numbers gives rise to a need for a constant expansion of capital equipment . . . in almost every branch of production. . . . In short, when numbers increase rapidly, there is need for a steady enlargement of <u>Productive Capacity</u>, in almost every part of the economic system.[1]

Thus arises the problem of an accession of productive equipment and productive capacity measured by the larger population. Natural resources represent only a potentiality, and their use depends to a great extent upon the availability of capital equipment. Only when import of capital equipment, industrial and agricultural machinery, pipes, water-boring machinery, and so on is expanding per capita and not only in the aggregate, and when an equilibrium is established between the added productive equipment and the larger population, can it be assumed that enlargement of productive capacity has kept pace with an increasing population and that economic growth was effective. Modern technology and capital-intensive industries make capital supply all the more important for the progress of young underdeveloped lands. The marginal capital/national product ratio in Israel in the years 1960-70 was 2.45 for the entire economy including housing and 1.75 not counting housing.

The interaction of population growth, its speed and volume, the intake of new capital, and the average per capita unit of capital is highly relevant to rise or fall in standards of living.[2] In an underdeveloped country with the complication of a rapid demographic advance, capital accumulation and formation cannot be quick enough to induce the needed expansion of productive capacity. That capacity should keep abreast of the growing number because a country's ability to absorb more citizens depends in large part upon its capital equipment and the level of education, skill, know-how, and technical talent of its producers.

At the same time, the flow of capital intended for new development and for lightening the stresses and strains on the economy in underdeveloped countries—to raise standards of living, to encourage international trade, and above all to expand the capacity of production—can be derived only from either formation by saving and accumulation or import. Financial conditions in Israel have been governed in the main by import of capital. When large sums are thus injected into a small economy, the influence is bound to be radical and plainly inflationary since inflation is generated directly by the injection if reserves of foreign currency rise and the increment is converted into local currency. In some periods, however restrictive the monetary policy, the resultant growth of money in circulation is so large in the small economy that its stimulus is very substantial: the new capital seeps through everywhere, and, the first and principal medium of its distribution is the building branch.

The increase of the labor force and the import and some formation of capital do not provide a complete explanation for the rate of growth which not only was quantitative but also caused a fundamental change in the economic structure of the country. As mentioned by Simon Kuznets, the direct contributions of man-hours and capital accumulation do not account for the total increase in the GNP. He attributes the residual increment "to an increase in efficiency in the productive resources—a rise in output per unit of input, due either to the improved quality of the resources, or to the effects of changing arrangements, or to the impact of technological change or to all three."[3]

Thus, economic growth is a comprehensive overall process in which expansionist forces of different weight, magnitude, and quality are being released and determine the pace of growth.

In Israel, the elements indicated by Kuznets certainly contributed substantially to economic growth because of the qualifications of a large segment of the population. However, the import of capital and the increase of population were so immense and condensed within a relatively short period of time that, although the other elements of growth cannot be disregarded or neglected, capital influx and increase of the labor force were decisive in maintaining such a high rate of real economic growth.

Economic growth at such a vigorous rate—10 percent per annum in real terms—over a period of more than twenty years testifies to an adequate supply of capital and level of investment. Indeed, a capital import of $10 billion over this period is evidence that the availability of capital did not impose a constraint on the expansion of the economy.

However, large capital imports could not be irrigated into fruition by a thin stream of immigrants nor could a rapid and numerous immigration mean an instant and effective expansion of demand unless accompanied by a copious capital flow. There is a certain optimum ratio between the factors that could, in theory, be reached at a point where their junction would make for the maximum economic growth with the minimum of inflation. Of course, that point is never attained in practice and the fluctuations of economic conditions depend partially on the degree of approximation to the optimum.

On the other hand, Israel's experience does not confirm the theory of the so-called "absorption capacity" for capital. A small country with a present population of about 3 million absorbed, during two decades (1950-70) some $10 billion and increased its GNP more than its growth of population of 134 percent during that period. The preconditions for such "absorption" are the availability of technical knowledge and its advantageous use and competitive ability with a view to penetrating export markets, as well as an institutional framework orientated toward economic growth.

Formation could be an alternative or supplementary source of capital to further economic growth. The first industrial revolution was based on a very high rate of savings and private accumulation of capital. The contemporary distribution of national income was instrumental in accelerating capital formation by assuring a high profitability and keeping wage rates at levels just sufficient for the maintenance and reproduction of the labor force. Those levels were possible because of the presence of a mass reserve of unemployed, a condition that

prevailed in a society of infant democracy with the bulk of the people
either inarticulate or without political influence. Totalitarianism re-
peated the performance: rapid industrialization and occupational reshuffle, establishment of heavy industry, and large-scale urbanization
could not have taken place without the quick formation of capital through
compulsory savings, and the regime was strong, stern, and severe
enough to enforce this manner of solving the problem of primary accumulation of capital. But that is an economic policy that can only be
carried through in a pre-democratic or totalitarian state by ruthless
methods of repression. Attempts to carry it through in a democratic
society have rarely succeeded and then only in countries where productivity rose rapidly, the rate of savings was unusually high, and
income did not rise too steeply.

A striking example of what can be achieved by capital import,
which served at least partly in lieu of primary formation of capital,
is provided by Israel's economic growth. Admittedly, its very rapid
achievement under a democratic and stable regime is due to several
factors, of which capital import is only one, although a significant one.
Political and security conditions, spiritual background, quality of human
material, the tension under which the effort was made—all these factors
shaped a unique set of circumstances. Import of capital did not by any
means entirely remove the need for policies that must be unpopular:
for some time, austerity had to be the rule, heavy taxation was levied,
and resources were diverted from consumption to investment. But,
patently, to have financed development of the Israel scope by internal
capital formation, if indeed it had been possible at all, would have
resulted in stresses and strains on the country's social and political
structure that have no precedent in history and would have proved
virtually unendurable.

The import of capital into Israel over a period of twenty-one
years bears witness to the truth of this contention. The inflow of
$10 billion made large-scale investment possible. The investment
was distributed among the branches of the economy as follows: 20.2
percent to industry, mining, and electricity; 11.6 percent to agriculture
and irrigation; 18.7 percent to transportation and communication;
30.6 percent to housing and building; and the balance of 18.9 percent
to trade and services. The capital was derived from a variety of
sources but the overwhelming proportion came from public and semipublic funds. These circumstances, rather than any preconceived
views, prompted and steered the planning of development and the
establishment of an order of priorities in investment. The import of
capital made it possible to dispense with any rapid internal accumulation of capital and to avoid a drastic lowering of living standards by
diversion of resources from consumption to investment. Moreover,
a substantial part of the capital imported did not entail capital charges

on account of principal and interest; this applies particularly to reparations and restitution funds from West Germany, gift funds raised
by Jewish communities all over the world, and U.S. government aid.

The nature of the imported capital provided wherewithal for
investment in the economic infrastructure. Because repayment of
capital and interest on these large sums was not required, investment
policy could be more daring and take extraordinary risks. In peopling
a country of meager natural wealth with immigrants from a hundred
countries, some of them backward, with low standards of education
and training, a certain waste of capital is inevitable. This was in the
main capital made available in the form of unrequited import. Public
funds coming to Israel are ready to accept risks that may involve
losses of capital values because they are collected specifically to
develop the state and, as such, are not hesitant, at least to some
degree, about being invested in less profitable enterprises.

Import of capital means import of capital goods and is reinforced
by import of consumer goods for the persons who are engaged in establishing the investment sector until the new capital yields new production, which has the effect either of diminishing imports for home
consumption or of expanding exports.

Capital imports into Israel appear to have provided an agent of
equilibrium between population growth and capital equipment. This
would seem to answer the requirement of Mombert that: "at the present
stage of economic development the necessary preliminary condition
for the absorptive capacity of an economy to keep pace with the increase of population is the yearly provision of new capital goods in
such quantities as to correspond at least to the average per capita of
the existing population."[4] Data available suggest that this is indeed
the condition that prevails in Israel.

Therefore, comigration produces a dual change in a country's
capacity to absorb additional population: the available space per in-
habitant is contracted but, on the other hand, the available capital
equipment is considerably augmented. The working of these divergent
factors on the approach to a hypothetical demographic optimum depends
largely on their quantitative ratio and interaction. Here, standard of
living and national income may serve as indicators.

THE ROLE OF PUBLIC CAPITAL

Governmental assistance in the form of long-term credits,
provision of land, and exemption from taxes and customs duties under
the Law for the Encouragement of Capital Investments played an

important part in Israel's rapid economic growth, and the state itself
invested extensively in the infrastructure, agriculture, irrigation,
industry, and housing. This large-scale official participation in economic development was imperative because private capital investment
was limited, while large amounts of imported public capital were
channeled through either the government or the Jewish Agency and its
subsidiaries. This capital—gift funds of Jewish communities in the
Diaspora, bonds issued by the government, reparations from West
Germany, credits from international institutions and banks—was used
partly to build up an infrastructure and adapt it to the needs of a quickly
expanding economy and partly for long-term financing of farm villages
or factories or for extending credits to private entrepreneurs, whether
individuals or companies, who also invested their own capital in this
development. The industrial sector of the labor economy, mainly
owned and managed by the Labour Federation, also was helped by
such credits.

The aggregate development expenditures of the government and
of the national institutions in the years 1948-71 were $4.7 billion.
Correlation between the investment of public funds and economic
growth was close and continuous throughout, amply attesting that the
activity of the public sector was very substantial in the process. The
extent, composition, and sources of capital invested by that sector
are functions of the fact that Israel, like other developing countries,
could not compete on a commercial basis on the capital markets of the
world with industrialized, highly-developed states.

The share of the state budget in Israel's GNP has been very
high from the start. Even if spells of war with their extraordinary
expenditure on defense are excluded, the average total share of the
state budget, including interest on the public debt, 25.5 percent during
the first decade and 32.1 percent in the years 1960-66; the corresponding shares of total current government revenue, excluding transfers
from abroad, were 22.7 and 29.4 percent. This large-scale official
spending was instrumental in furthering economic development through
special development budgets, and it was substantially supplemented
by the outlays of local authorities and the Jewish Agency, which in
the main financed agricultural settlement but also invested in a variety
of economic undertakings, such as shipping and housing.

Much import of capital and large investment spared Israel the
ordeal of grappling with the grave problem of disequilibrium between
capital import and investment and increment of population. Investments stemming from import of public capital stimulated and hastened
economic growth, frequently in conjunction with private capital, even
if part of the capital was lost in the process because of lack of experience, know-how, and administrative ability or due to inefficiency.

Import of capital alone does not suffice to finance development anywhere, and in the less-developed countries voluntary private savings are rather low as a rule; to speed up progress, developing countries must have recourse to compulsory savings by means of taxation. For quicker formation of capital, governments interested in their countries' economic growth are bound to obtain foreign governmental and international aid and channel it through their budgets and, at the same time, to compel savings through high taxes, which also increase those budgets. This partly explains the correlation between the large proportion of state expenditure in the GDP and rapid economic growth.

At the outset of development, much of the investment goes to build up the economic infrastructure and public services, for which private capital usually is not forthcoming. In that first phase of development and economic growth, a large inflow of goods with a fairly high tariff in force raises government revenue.

The multiplication and extension of government services mean the employment of a large cadre of medical personnel, teachers, and administrators, magnifying their component in the labor force of the public sector and its weight in the economy.

Government investment, out of its total budget, in the economy of Israel has been high, clearly manifesting a disposition to quicken growth by large official participation in view of the inadequacy of private capital. Outside aid injected into the economy through government channels is one aspect of this development; another is the mobilization of capital through financial institutions, such as pension and other funds, which was promoted by the government for investment purposes.

CAPITAL FORMATION AND SAVINGS

The problem that arises is to find noninflationary sources of capital for investment. Therefore, it is essential to first analyze the process of capital formation, which encountered many difficulties.

Israel is a country of scarce natural resources. The democratic regime lends backing to strong pressures and claims for a higher standard of living. Since the income accruing to factors of production from the greater real output of the economy was used overwhelmingly for consumption, the share of the added output left over to finance investment was insubstantial. Such a situation results in fewer exports and more imports. It follows that a higher level of savings was a vital condition for the channeling of the increment in the GNP to productive investment or to an improvement of the balance of payments.

Another problem inseparable from development in Israel is the high rate of public dissavings due, inter alia, to defense expenditure and the cost of immigrant absorption, and made possible by what the public sector receives from abroad. A study done by a French expert, Edmond Lisle, shows that family savings in Israel in recent years have been about the same as in other countries.[5] The rate of household savings in Israel in 1957-58 came to 5 percent of disposable income per annum, or pretty well, on a par with most of the West. The most widespread form of savings was in housing, although in recent years investments in financial assets have risen considerably, probably also because of the availability of government securities linked to foreign currency or the cost-of-living index.

The report of the Bank of Israel for 1963 discusses the problem of private and public savings:

> In comparing the rate of saving in Israel with that in other countries, it should be remembered that the large volume of unilateral transfer receipts from abroad depresses the rate of saving from national income. Such transfers lead to a rise in consumption expenditure, thus reducing saving out of national income. This applies to every one of the sectors.
>
> Personal restitution payments from West Germany definitely increase consumption spending in the private sector. When the incremental consumption is netted out of the domestic income of the private sector, its savings out of such income is low. This is true for the public sector and non-profit institutions as well, and is especially significant in respect of the latter in view of the large weight of foreign transfer receipts in their total income.[6]

A comparison of the rate of national saving in Israel with the rate elsewhere is relevant:

> The rate for Israel during the years 1957-60 came to 3.7 percent—a rate exceeded by all other countries except Panama and Peru. The reason for the low level of national saving in Israel is the big weight of unilateral transfers. Whereas in the other countries national saving is actually the amount saved out of the total resources at the disposal of the economy, the situation is different in Israel, where unrequited transfers during the period discussed amounted to 13 percent of national income. These transfer payments have a marked effect on consumption in particular; it is

largely because of this factor that the national saving is low
as compared with other countries.

In the private sector unrequited transfers do not have
such a marked effect. Personal restitution receipts, the
main component item in such transfers, constituted in
1960 only some 6 percent of disposable private income
from domestic sources. In addition, these are largely
one-time receipts and the marginal propensity to consume
receipts of this type is relatively low.[7]

A steady upward curve in the rate of savings was perceptible
throughout the decade 1960-70, but on the whole the contribution of
capital formation and savings to economic development was neither
large nor far-reaching.

STRUCTURAL CHANGES OF THE ECONOMY

The large import of capital made possible a better and greater
use of existing resources, which is of particular consequence where
those resources are scarce. Interchangeability of capital, space,
and other resources is of overriding importance, especially in view
of the correlation between capital investment and productivity: development turns on supply of capital, and immigration and the lending
of capital are interdependent:

As far back as 1885 Sir Robert Giffen pointed out that:
. . . in the earlier years of prosperity a considerable
lending of capital from old to new countries goes on, and
this lending of capital promotes emigration from the old
countries to the new, helping to give greater employment
for labour in the new countries than there would otherwise be.[8]

But capital flows to areas that are rich in resources. Thus, it
was unlikely that the substitution in Israel of capital for space and the
rest would be a natural outcome of strictly economic conditions and
considerations. There is also the unavoidable write-off of part of the
investment in transplantation and settlement:

The hidden costs of migration and development are consistently ignored. The cost of the transfer of population and
of equipment of the territory do not cover all the costs by
any means. The loss of time arising in the handling of
capital sums by persons unaccustomed to it, the unlearning
of the lessons learned in other lands, and the learning

of lessons applicable to a new country, all involve costs
and loss which are rarely taken into calculations. The
migrant is forced to handle a series of problems indi-
vidually, which the growing community has had to tackle
collectively. The settler is always, so far as his own
problem is concerned, in the difficult position of the
pioneer.[9]

Once more, it is seen that transportation to an area whose scanty
resources must be offset by larger capital equipment, as is the case
in Israel, is feasible only if capital import is set and kept moving by
extra-economic factors, and a lot of the capital must be public because
some will be lost in the process.

The conclusions drawn from these premises are set forth in a
report of the International Labour Office:

It may be concluded that a revival of settlement movements,
and particularly of migration for settlement, which official
services and settlement organizations of the social type are
at present not sufficiently developed to bring about, cannot
be expected to result from the action of commercial and
speculative settlement bodies.

Such a revival can be obtained only in the measure in
which it is found possible to develop and multiply organizations prepared to invest the necessary capital, granting
sufficiently long periods for repayment, and able to create
in the settler's mind the certainty that every effort will be
made to insure his success.[10]

Transition to a modern capital-intensive economy has its effect
on occupational distribution: added capital equipment should conduce
to a more efficient division of labor and speed up that transition, and
changes in occupational distribution, which are their concomitant,
bear on economic growth by giving secondary and tertiary incomes
a greater share in national income. The importance of space and
natural resources is thereby lessened and other factors round which
economic growth revolves increase in their relative weight.

The Malthusian theory can no longer be crudely applied, and
inquiry into the interrelation of economic structure and occupational
distribution is essential. Diversification of demand, consequent upon
higher incomes, enlarges the part of secondary and tertiary stages of
production. There must be fewer producers in the primary stage if
their output capacity is rising; otherwise, no market would be found
for what they make except by an extraordinary expansion of exports,

which rarely occurs. Thus, the choice is between many primary producers with low output capacity, as in less advanced countries, or few with a high output capacity, as in more developed ones.

Klonov has established "that a decline in the percentage of the agricultural population and an increase in the industrial population lead to an increase in the productivity of the soil and of agricultural labor."[11] The link here is with expansion of urban markets for farm produce.

The structural changes in an economy due to modernization and a transfer from primary sources of production (agriculture) to secondary (industry) and tertiary (services) will raise standards of living and consumption on all levels of society but may sharpen professional and social differentiations. Table 16 shows the alterations in the several branches of Israel's labor force.

An accretion of capital equipment changed the economic structure of Israel in two ways: (1) it superimposed an industrialized system of production on the old economy, enlarging the part of secondary and tertiary income by reason of division of labor and (2) it provided new openings for employment which, in turn, called forth the required labor force.

TABLE 16

Breakdown of Labor Force by Economic Branch,
1955, 1960, 1966, and 1969
(percentages)

Branch	1955	1960	1966	1969
Agriculture	17.6	17.3	12.3	10.5
Industry	21.9	23.2	26.1	26.2
Construction	9.3	9.3	8.7	8.2
Electricity, water	2.0	2.2	2.0	1.9
Commerce, banking	13.5	12.3	13.0	12.9
Transportation, communication	6.2	6.2	6.6	7.7
Personal services	21.2	22.0	23.3	24.5
Public services	8.3	7.5	8.0	8.1
Total	100.0	100.0	100.0	100.0

Here the quality of the immigrant population is most material. The bulk of the immigrant population had to undergo an occupational reshuffle. This occupational reshuffle and the economic growth that followed were facilitated by the availability of a nucleus of highly skilled labor—technicians, experts, scientists, manufacturers with overseas experience, designers, engineers, agronomists, diamond cutters and polishers, horticulturists, irrigation engineers, and the like—that could apply the quickening industrial and agricultural techniques and thus supply the essential precondition of rising productivity and economic growth.

As industrialization spread and the economy was modernized, there was an expansion of the population stratum engaged in commerce, the professions, the distributive trades, and the state machinery itself, thus bringing into being a superstructure over the basic callings of agriculture and industry. But population growth reacts favorably on agricultural output and industrial concentration alike if the proportion of secondary and tertiary producers rises:

> The natural capacity of secondary industries to maintain and absorb population depends not only on the resources available, but upon the extent to which the home market has become large enough to provide opportunities for large scale production, and upon the use made of these opportunities. Natural growth is progressive and accumulative.[12]

A transformation of that sort took place, gradually and slowly to be sure, in certain developing countries. Its mechanism is as follows: The expansion of the manufacturing industry is not limited by such constraints as a shortage of land and other natural resources; know-how, managerial and labor skills, and capital per worker determine the output per capita. The concentration of industry and economies of scale stimulate the process of growth and increase productivity per unit of output. To some extent, this also applies to services, such as transportation.[13] As already noted, the process is linked intimately with marketing facilities. Its pace can be quickened and it can take on the character of an economic revolution if the entire structure of an economy is built within a short space of time, as Israel's experience proves. The assumptions that "economic progress clearly can be made by increasing product per head in the sphere of primary, secondary and tertiary industry; or by transferring labor from less to more productive spheres" and that "generally speaking, the main dynamic of economic advances has been rising income per head in either secondary or tertiary industry, often in both, and the transfer of population away from primary industry"[14] are upheld by the experience of Israel demonstrating that the higher per capita income in the secondary and tertiary stages of production and the higher percentage of population engaged in secondary and tertiary industries have raised the standard of living.

Thus, the new strata of population laid down by accretion of capital are the outcome of structural and socioeconomic changes that work upon the whole economy, shifting it from a subsistence to an exchange economy. There are, of course, reservations. If consequential economic growth is to be achieved, the capital import must be swift and voluminous; it must be invested in productive assets, not hoarded, and its use in that way based on sound economic analyses of opportunities and a proper order of priorities. If all these conditions are present, there can be a breakthrough to self-perpetuating sustained growth, again testifying to the functional nexus between capital investment and the rate of that growth.

The case of Israel goes to show that economic growth of speed and continuity can be realized in a democracy, provided that a large inflow of capital, allowing for a slower tempo of internal capital formation, is at its disposal for a sufficiently long time. If the imponderables, which play so important a role in Israel, also are taken into account, it seems reasonable to draw certain universal conclusions from the case.

Large-scale investment led to horizontal and vertical changes in the economic structure, a far-reaching occupational redistribution, higher standards of living, and a new relationship between the number of workers and the investment assets—namely, a transition to a capital-intensive economy. In every case, of course, what is material is how investment is made up, be economic branches.

From 1950-70, the real annual level of investment rose three-fold. Its composition markedly reflects trends and processes that typify Israel's economy. The percentage invested in agriculture, including irrigation, corresponds to that in developed countries, even though in Israel the capital investment in agriculture is on the whole high by comparison. The percentage invested in industry and transportation is an index of an ever-growing industrialization, while the fairly low percentage going to commerce and services is an index of a labor-intensive branch that requires little capital. The high percentage invested in construction is of special interest: it is obviously explained by mass immigration. In the beginning, it greatly influences future economic growth because the expanding branch is one that is free of marketing problems by virtue of mass immigration and import of capital to finance it. The larger local market under the thrust of widespread construction encourages more production to supply other needs, and a production that lags behind added purchasing power is an incentive to expand all branches to supply what the local market needs. Thus, in Israel the spark passed between the two poles: capital and greater demand of newcomers possessed of imported purchasing power. An expanded market attracts new industries.

Imported capital, public or private, seizes investment opportunities if there is an outlet for the products of the proliferating mechanism of production, and those products look chiefly to the home market, which is partly dependent on the extra buying capacity generated by investments in building. It has been seen that it is easier to absorb a large number of immigrants at one time because a restricted inflow will not establish a home market with the technical and economic minima that are essential to the setting up of new plants. But two factors—the natural limitations of every country in respect of its resources and the difficulties in its balance of payments, which are certain to emerge in the course of time—must always be borne in mind in any evaluation of economic growth in those circumstances. Massive imports of capital may conceal the existence of this problem for a long while, but it must manifest itself eventually and indeed it is the central problem of Israel's economy.

The question of investment policy arises: the capital made available on such terms is nonrecurrent, which necessitates selectivity and in regard to every project it must be asked whether there is no better alternative use of briefly available and limited resources. In a wholly free economy, the micro- and macro-economic aspects are tightly interwoven, but where there is state invervention and an element of state direction a scale of priorities is required and investment must satisfy two criteria: (1) its influence on the balance of payments, taking into account the price in local currency of the dollar saved by producing an import substitute or the added value of what is produced for export, and (2) its profitability by micro-economic standards.

To choose between alternatives is especially difficult where the share of public investment is large. There is a dual reason for this: the weight of pressure groups and the propensity of political institutions to disregard the limitations of every economic act, and the impossibility of achieving the totality of desiderata without harming the economy and nullifying the very purpose for which investments are made.

NOTES

1. R. R. Kuczynski, T. H. Marshall, A. M. Carr-Saunders, H. B. Henderson, and Arnold Plant, The Population Problem, the Experts and the Public (London: George Allen and Unwin Ltd., 1938), pp. 88, 89.

2. League of Nations, World Economic Survey, 1938/39 (Geneva), p. 159.

3. Simon Kuznets, Modern Economic Growth (New Haven and London: Yale University Press, 1966), pp. 80-81.

4. Grundriss der Sozialökonomik, II (Tubingen: Verlag I. C. B. Mohr, 1914), p. 79.

5. Edmond A. Lisle, "Household Savings in Israel, 1954-1957/58." In Bank of Israel Bulletin (Jerusalem: April, 1964).

6. Bank of Israel, Annual Report 1963, p. 392.

7. Ibid., pp. 406-7.

8. Fergus Chalmers Wright, Population and Peace, (Paris: International Institute of Intellectual Cooperation, League of Nations, 1939), p. 257, quoting International Labour Office reports: "The Migration of Workers: .Recruitment, Placing and Conditions of Labour." Studies reports: Series 0 (Migration), No. 5, 1936.

9. Institute of Pacific Relations, The Peopling of Australia, Series No. 4 (Melbourne: Melbourne University Press, 1933), p. 263.

10. Technical Conference of Experts, Technical and Financial International Cooperation with Regard to Migration for Settlement, Studies and Reports Series (Migration) No. 7, (Geneva: International Labour Office, 1938), pp. 32, 71.

11. Klonov, "Recherches Statistiques sur la Relation entre la Productivité Agricole et la Densité et la Structure de la Population." Quoted in Imre Ferenczi, The Synthetic Optimum of Population (Paris: League of Nations, 1938), p. 31.

12. Institute of Pacific Relations, op. cit., p. 117.

13. Wright, op. cit., p. 288.

14. Colin Clark, The Conditions of Economic Progress (London: Macmillan and Co. Ltd., 1940), pp. 11, 12.

THE HUMAN FACTOR IN THE
DEVELOPMENT OF ISRAEL

Israel's principal demographic and economic question is whether a population increment of 134 percent in the two decades 1950-1970 has been fully absorbed, whether it struck roots in the country's economy, and what the mechanics of this process are.

Mainly by immigration, the labor force multiplied from 427,000 in 1950 to 1,001,300 in 1970, a multiplication essential for economic growth since without it capital investment can cause a shortage of manpower, which in fact happened in the years 1968-70, although the labor force rose by some 7.3 percent during that interval. It is noteworthy that this rapid rise did not add to unemployment except in the first years of the Israeli state; on the contrary, the curve of employment climbed steadily, parallel with immigration and with the expansion of productive forces; unemployment generally was in inverse ratio to immigration.

The Israel experiment, as far as it goes, confirms by every practical and empirical test the conclusions of theoretical analysis. The transformation of the economy by a comigration of capital and labor, extensive building, new marketing possibilities, and the ensuing growth of production show how immigration creates its own conditions of economic absorption and how economic conditions may become a function of the process of migration. Thus, the proportion of labor to economic factors determines the degree of employment or unemployment.

The contribution of Israel's force to economic growth was not confined to rising numbers. Output per worker has increased at an average annual rate of 5.3 percent, reflecting a broader basis of capital equipment as well as advances in managerial skill and workers' productivity, and economies of scale. Skill and knowledge are a factor of no little consequence in the set of conditions that make for industrial development. Their absence, conversely, is an obstacle to industrial- ization in colonial countries. Thus, "Modern machine industry depends in a peculiar degree on education, and the attempt to build it up with an illiterate body of workers must be difficult and perilous."[1]

Israel's potential of know-how was augmented by the combined effect the foundation and swift enlargement of institutions of elementary, secondary, and higher education, laboratories, libraries, and so on, supported by the government and by overseas sponsors, and by the spread of scientific knowledge. These resources were not formed or applied by or through immigration alone; they were extended and enriched by education and training and by state policies designed to enlarge the supply of instructed, schooled, and skilled labor and to impart technological knowledge. A comparison with a number of de- veloping and developed countries makes it is evident that in respect to literacy Israel belongs to the class of developed nations (see Table 17).

The 43,000 men and women enrolled in Israel's universities today make the country's student-population ratio the third highest in the world. UNESCO's 1969 Statistical Yearbook gives the following data on the number of students per 100,000 inhabitants; in the United States, 3,471; in Canada, 2,201; in Israel, 1,488 (in 1966); in Japan, 1,398; in Sweden, 1,250; in France, 1,239; in Lebanon, 1,156; in Great Britain, 716; in West Germany, 695; in Egypt, 565. The pro- portion of graduates in science and technology in Israel's civilian labor force—10 for every 10,000 in 1967—is also very high globally, comparable to that of the United States, Great Britain, and Japan, and exceeding that in Canada, France, Holland, and Belgium.

Israel has seven university-type institutions of higher learning that confer academic degrees. One of their major functions is to train manpower for scientific research and for faculty cadres; some 52 percent of Israel's scientists and technologists were trained in Israel. Applied research is concerned mainly with agriculture, water, chemicals, geology, and electronics. In the last few years, there has been a marked rise in industrial research and developmental activity, largely under the stimulus of increased state spending for these purposes.

All this has a powerful impact on economic growth, particularly in the secondary stage since the location of many factories is in- creasingly governed by such factors as industrial milieu, which com- prises more than the mere availability of skilled labor and is connected

TABLE 17

Literacy and School
Attendance in Selected Countries

Country	Year	Adult Literacy Rate	School Enrollment Ratios (adjusted)
Israel	1965	94	82
Iraq	1965	14	50
Iran	1967	23	45
Tunisia	1965	16	62
Egypt	1965	20	52
Turkey	1965	38	54
Yugoslavia	1965	76	78
Bulgaria	1965	85	88
Italy	1968	92	72
Poland	1965	95	88
France	1968	96	95
Japan	1968	98	92
United States	1968	98	93
U.S.S.R.	1965	98	82

with science and knowledge, research laboratories and training schools, tradition, and managerial ability and techniques:

Subsidiary trades grow up, testing and research laboratories and training schools are established near by, buyers come regularly from a distance, and different firms can draw upon the same pool of trained labor with less unoccupied reserve. In many industries economies of this type depend upon the large market made possible by world trade.[2]

The importance of this concentration is signalized positively and negatively.

Thus, as noted, immigration movements have more than once been the positive precursors of industrial growth by transmitting skills from a country of origin to a country of absorption, but they can also have a negative impact as in Spain, which exemplifies a country in decline owing to the expulsion of the valuable manpower that is a precondition of industrial development:

Spain is a case in point. She undertook, more
systematically than most of the West European nations,
to control the type of her population. The Moors, her
industrious and prosperous but religiously and racially
heterodox citizens, she expelled in the interest of
racial and religious unity. The undesigned result was
the destruction of the possibility of industrial development. In the interest of religion and the redistribution
of financial power, she expelled the Jews with results
disastrous to her business and commercial prosperity.
("The ruin of Spain may be chiefly traced to the expulsion or extirpation of her Moorish, Jewish and
heretical subjects.") And, finally, and again in the
interest of a decadent religious orthodoxy, she des-
troyed her intellectuals and thereby insured herself
a long period of religious orthodoxy and intellectual
stagnation.

No less meaningful for Israel's economic growth were the imponderables of history, nationhood, and society. These imponderables,
and a dedication that sprang from the hopes and aspirations deeply
embedded in the national soul, are vitally important although they do
not lend themselves to quantitative measurement. The threat of
physical destruction, a national singleness of purpose, the sense of
grim necessity and historical mission, the psychology of siege "with
our backs to the sea" all were instrumental in giving a tremendous
thrust to the work of reconstruction.

Transplantation of population is in large part controlled by the
economic absorptive capacity of the country of immigration. But this
capacity is an undefined and hardly definable concept; it is extremely
doubtful that it can ever be gauged in fixed arithmetical terms; it is
the function of many variables which in turn depend on the specific
experience of each country. The equilibrium of the components of an
economy in their dynamic interaction, as well as technical culture
and such social relations as the distribution of wealth and income,
affect the ability of any country to support its inhabitants at a reasonable and rising standard of living.

The make-up of immigration to Israel was well-adapted to the
shift to secondary and tertiary stages of production; the traditional
Jewish mobility and versatility may have made the process easier
and speedier, as an Arab-Lebanese author has recognized:

In recent years, large numbers of Jews have migrated to Palestine because changes in political
conditions in Europe have seriously threatened their

erstwhile means of livelihood, and their political and
even personal liberties. Such migrations to escape
persecutions are numerous in history, and are usually
remarkable, not for their numerical greatness, but
for the superior quality of the human material involved,
and the benefits which the refugees from persecution
have brought to their country of adoption. [3]

Once more it can be seen how immigration impelled by extra-economic
pressures turns out to be an especially fertile source of population
that is sufficiently diversified in its vocations and highly productive.
Nowhere else aside from Greece, was a transplantation of such
dimensions as in Israel the result of "pushing" forces. The transplantation of population to Israel was entirely on the lines of such
early migrations as those of the Huguenots and Puritans who fled
from religious and political persecutions; this aspect, and the economy of a growing population, were the hall-marks of the transplantation to Israel.

Industrialization and rural modernization were made possible
by the natural endowments and acquired skills of the newcomers in
unison with import of capital to furnish the means of production. [4]
To be sure, as has been noted, not all newcomers but only those from
the highly-developed and industrialized countries possessed the essential qualifications, but the proportion was still large enough, linked
with the education and training efforts for those lacking them, to lift
the economic level as a whole and speed up qualitative and quantitative
expansion.

To be successful, transplantation necessarily presupposes a
rising productivity per worker on the land, in factories, and in every
other economic branch and, correlated with rising productivity, a
higher standard of living and a greater demographic density. Higher
capital investment per worker and higher productivity invariably
mean higher per capita incomes, whence flows a diversified demand
for goods and services that, in turn, enlarges the output of manufac-
tured goods in general and of commodities in more elastic demand
in particular.

Higher productivity per man-day of labor would be the direct
consequence of more intensive use of productive resources. In all
periods, population density has been determined in part by historical
and economic factors; natural conditions have never completely explained the difference between areas. The freeing of population
potentialities from a too close dependence on natural resources is
a trend accentuated by the development of modern technology. The
essence of present economic progress is a swing in the pendulum of

factors conditioning economic absorptive capacity. The almost physiocratic idea of absorptive capacity, linking it tightly to available space and natural resources, does not square with present circumstances. With agriculture no longer the central branch in progressive communities, natural resources are less consequential in restricting absorptive capacity. Many new physical and economic factors, each with a direct bearing on absorptive capacity and the possibility of consciously shaping conditions through economic policy, must now be taken into account, and historical, economic, and social criteria applied to the process of absorbing immigration. That space and natural resources are receding in importance as against the new factors is not proof that, the greater the density, the closer the approach to an optimum population; this development only sustains the thesis, with Israel as the case in point, that absorptive capacity is a relative concept. The question arises as to how seriously a dearth of natural resources can constrain economic growth: in the final analysis, it boils down to the interchangeability of natural wealth with human resources of capital, skill, know-how, and technology.

CAPACITY OF ABSORPTION

Any calculation of a country's capacity to absorb immigrants is bound to be confined to the immediate future, whether the point of departure is consumption and marketing prospects or expansion of production. Each phase of development brings new and unpredictable problems and possibilities. Sismondi says: "The true problem of the statesman is to find the combination and the ratio of population to wealth which will assure most happiness to the human race on a given area."[5]

The complex character of the modern economy makes that task exceedingly difficult. Mutation of economic conditions, technical discovery and invention, development of potential resources, and shifts in consumption and market must all be considered. Such elements as capital and scientific and technical knowledge are subject to almost endless change. In a country where rapid immigration is conjoined with import of capital and skills, the factors of cultural and technical levels, economic and social systems, structure and quality of population and occupational distribution, and the dynamic interaction of all these factors are infinite in their variety.

Experience (Japan, Hong Kong, Israel) and theoretical analysis indicate that physical conditions and material resources are decreasing in importance and in their impact on economic growth while background and economic and social conditions play an immensely important role in conditioning population growth and economic expansion.[6]

The interaction of population and physical background, and their repercussions on one another, cannot be disregarded. To the same extent that a country's absorptive capcity is determined by its attributes, those same attributes are transformed by the very growth of population, by its character, proclivities, efficiency, and energy. These are the most bountiful sources that any nation can command, and they determine how far it is possible to exploit the natural resources and productive powers of this country or that to satisfy the economic needs of man. [7]

The density of population or the relation of the number of inhabitants to the surface area was used in different periods to measure a country's human saturation, but modern economic theory arrived at the conclusion "that there is no magnitude expressible in exact figures that is in constant ratio to the relatively exact figure of the population of a given region, "[8] and there is empirical proof that natural conditions are not the chief indicator of demographic developments. The problem is put in a nutshell in the following analysis by Erich W. Zimmermann:

> Population trends, however, must always be considered in conjunction with, or in relation to, cultural development. Numbers of people by themselves mean little: but numbers equipped with a certain knowledge, endowed with certain abilities, supported by "horse power", handicapped by certain inhibitions, are vital. Moreover, population trends rather than population status must be considered: the treatment must be dynamic, not static. [9]

Experience bears out the view that some of the factors "which influence the distribution and density of population are, in part at least, susceptible to control by organized human effort. "[10] The idea of an optimum population holding good for all time therefore must be rejected. It is now recognized that, even if the optimum is exceeded, it may be restored by capital accumulation and technical progress. [11]

When agriculture was the predominant occupation, it was less difficult to assess economic absorptive capacity for a growing population: of necessity, the starting point was the level of basic natural resources—land area and fertility, both more in the nature of constants rather than variables. But as agriculture advanced even that physical foundation underwent greater changes: such modern farming methods as rotation of crops, irrigation, fertilization, development of new strains congenial to soil that had long been considered uncultivable, and recently what is known as the "Green Revolution," heralding new strains of wheat, rice, and sorghum, have transformed many accepted standards.

The frequency with which migration is directed from sparsely to densely populated areas supports the conclusions of statistical analysis. Walter F. Willcox cites the progressive tempo of Italian emigration by districts and seeks to explain the exodus from under-populated areas by purely historical and economic factors divorced from natural conditions. He arrives at the conclusion that those factors stimulated migration from agricultural to industrializing areas. The highest rate of emigration was registered for sparsely populated areas. This shows the falsity of the prevailing opinion that there is a direct relation between emigration and density. In fact, no such relation exists and in many cases the reverse is found. [12]

Japan went through a similar experience. In 1925, a comparison was made of the density in Japan and other countries, and the figures seemed to signify overpopulation in Japan. [13] But in his analysis of the Japanese population, W. R. Crocker points out that already in the 1920's there was a spectacular rise in standards of life in that country, and he stresses the fact that production far outpaced the growth of population. [14] After nearly half a century this analysis has proved remarkably exact, for Japan today is the third industrial power in the world, with an annual per capita income of $1,300, token of a high level of economic development despite scarcity of natural resources.

An extreme case is Hong Kong, which is virtually devoid of natural resources and must rely on imports for its vital needs, including part of the water supply, and which crowds a population of four million in an area less than 5 percent that of Israel. For all that, Hong Kong enjoys full employment, an economic boom, and, after Japan, the largest per capita income in East Asia. Admittedly, this is a freak case because of the proximity of a Chinese giant interested in entreport trade. This proviso, however, does not detract from the corroboration that Hong Kong offers of the evidence that human and natural resources are more and more interchangeable in economic growth.

But natural resources, agricultural apart, do play a more important role. To begin with, the arable areas are not unalterably limited but can be changed by artificial facts, and new land can be brought under the plough by reclamation, drainage, terracing, and irrigation, in short, by applying capital to the soil. The development of secondary and tertiary stages of production has little if anything to do with population density. It will be asked whether the presence of natural resources provides a test of the capacity of a given area to maintain its population. Here, certain theoretical considerations arise. Natural resources can hardly be considered as indicative of the capacity of a country to support an expanding population. The static concept of a constant base of natural resources is, in the light of experience, an obvious fallacy. The dynamic aspect of resources is more important than the static and what counts are not only the actual but the potential resources. [15]

Another flaw of the criterion in natural resources is that some that are of growing importance in the modern economy can never be quantified, such as skill, knowledge, and capital. [16]

It is essentially the subjective qualities of its human material that determines a country's capacity for economic growth:

> It is probable that one of the reasons why those
> countries which lie upon the principal channels of
> commerce have developed their economies relatively
> rapidly is to be found in that ferment of ideas which
> accompanied the intermingling of peoples and the inter-
> change of commodities. [17]

This "ferment of ideas" is an imponderable that can never be reckoned with in any static conception of economic absorption. Thus, it seems to be true that "the quality of the population, and more particularly the ratio which the skilled and trained population bears to the whole, is becoming more important."[18]

Moreover, economic capacity and growth are plainly affected by the equilibrium of the components of an economy in dynamic interaction, in their technical, cultural, and social interlocking, such as distribu-tion of wealth and income.

An increment of output per man-day of labor flows straight from fuller use of productive resources. In that context, Paul Mombert holds that, wherever technique and economy have come to a certain degree of development and population has reached a period of co-operation and interaction and its growing numbers permit natural resources to be more thoroughly utilized, individual productivity goes up as the population rises. [19] This is particularly true in coun-tries that are forced to circumvent the effects of the law of diminish-ing returns by changing over to lines of production where larger in-vestment of capital and labor gives higher income and where larger populations often mean greater yield of capital. This may be the explanation of the phenomenon upon which Colin Clark comments: the high productivity of Denmark and the Netherlands and the low pro-ductivity of some sparsely populated areas. The most striking evi-dence of high productivity correlated with high density of population is provided by Japan. [20] Last but not least, the flexibility of con-ditions conducive to economic growth is demonstrated in the case of Israel, a country with a pronounced scarcity of natural resources and an outstanding record of rapid economic development.

Thus, analysis of density in its bearing on capacity to support a given population establishes that "the population capacity of the land depends . . . on the total available resources that land, people, science, technology, and market demand, . . . make possible in combinations that are largely unique from region to region and from country to country."[21]

Historical development best and comprehensively explains divergence in density. Primitive or progressive social systems, civil or national wars, colonial expeditions and conquests are all part of what decides which shall be the thickly and which the thinly peopled areas of the world, but of course only, within obvious physical bounds— extreme cold or heat, deserts and jungles fall outside them. But granted soil that can be tilled and a tolerable climate, it is the forces of history in mounting measure that make and modify economic absorptive capacity, with the forces of nature of progressively diminishing importance. In this gradual release of population potential from too irksome a vassalage to natural resources, the developments of the machine age count a great deal, contributing as they do to shifts and changes in the significance of the factors that condition economic growth and the capacity for it. These incidences, their respective weights and reciprocity, must be detected and assessed, and discussion centered on ways and means of consciously molding conditions through economic policy.[22]

Again it is clear that economic development today is typified by the variation in importance of its agents: it is now not natural conditions but human resources that count decisively.

On the strength of the foregoing conclusions, the only way of calculating economic absorption capacity that suggests itself is to analyze, economically and empirically, the conditions and directions of development and of factors within the body economic making for equilibrium or dislocation, for progress or regression.

Israel's experience corroborates these general conclusions. The wide disparity between the scarcity of natural resources and limitations of space and water on the one hand and the rapid growth of the economy and population on the other is clearly reflected by all of the country's economic indicators. Subsequent developments contradicted and disproved virtually all forecasts of the economic future of Palestine under the Mandate, and all Israel, based on evaluations of its potential resources, some of them by unbiased experts.

The rate of economic growth achieved by Israel and the degree of economic integration of the immigrant population, despite the country's natural handicaps, together with the contradiction between its predicted potentialities and the present realities, provide a test of the interchangeability of human and material resources.

NOTES

1. Harold Butler, Problems of Industry in the East, with special Reference to India, French India, Ceylon, Malaya and the Netherlands Indies, (Geneva: International Labour Office, 1938), p. 24.

2. Eugene Staley, World Economy in Transition, (New York: Council on Foreign Relations, 1939), p. 248. See Alfred Marshall, Principles of Economics (London: Macmillan and Co. Ltd., 1922), p. 271.

3. S. B. Himadeh, ed., Economic Organization of Palestine (Beirut: American University, 1936), p. 20.

4. Staley, op. cit., p. 279.

5. J. C. L. S. de Sismondi: Nouveaux Principes d'Economie Politique Vol. II, Chapter VII.

6. Frederick Chalmers Wright, Population and Peace, (Paris: International Institute of Intellectual Cooperation, League of Nations, 1939), p. 72.

7. Paul Mombert, "Wirtschaft und Bevölkerung," in Grundriss der Sozialökonomik, II (Tübingen: Verlag I. C. B. Mohr, 1914), pp. 33, 67, 69.

8. Wright, op. cit., p. 79.

9. Erich W. Zimmermann, World Resources and Industries: An Appraisal of Agricultural and Industrial Resources (New York: Harper and Bros., 1933), pp. 122-23.

10. C. B. Fawcett, "Some Factors in Population Density," in G. H. L. F. Pitt Rivers, ed., Problems of Population, the Report of the Proceedings of the Second General Assembly of the International Union for the Scientific Investigation of Population Problems (London, 1931), p. 197.

11. D. V. Glass, Population Policies and Movements in Europe (London: Oxford University Press, 1940), pp. 369-70.

12. Walter F. Willcox, ed., International Migrations (New York, 1929), pp. 477-78.

13. League of Nations, Population and Natural Resources (Geneva, 1927).

14. W. R. Crocker, The Japanese Population Problem, the Coming Crisis, (London: George Allen and Unwin Ltd., 1931), p. 53.

15. W. B. Hurd, "The Ability of Canada to Receive Immigration" in H. F. Angus, Canada and the Doctrine of Peaceful Change (mimeographed).

16. Staley, op. cit., p. 292.

17. N. F. Hall, Preliminary Investigation into Measures of National or International Character for Raising the Standard of Living, memorandum prepared by N. F. Hall (League of Nations: 1938), p. 48.

18. Ibid., p. 87.

19. Mombert, op. cit., p. 69.

20. Colin Clark, The Conditions of Economic Progress, (London: Macmillan and Co. Ltd., 1940), pp. 245-46.

21. Staley, op. cit., p. 100.

22. Zimmerman, op. cit., p. 124.

6

ECONOMIC GROWTH
AND
THE MECHANICS
OF
TRANSPLANTATION

It has been pointed out that in Israel's case the causal link between economic growth and population transplantation and capital influx is forged by an intake of skill, know-how, and money. What, then, is the mechanism of the process?

Analysis in time series shows that each new wave of immigration sweeps in on a broader basis and so expands the framework of the economy but improvement in the standard of living persists even if peak numbers of immigration cannot be sustained. The undulation of economic life that is a concomitant of migration thus brings about a double expansion: horizontally of the population and vertically of incomes, accompanied by a rise in standards of living and consumption, that is, ultimately a rise in effective demand conducing to a very great extension of markets and by its repercussions stimulating the growth of production.

Indexes of Israel's production, consumption, and capital import testify that the growth of population, in the main a product of immigration, was associated with an expansion of capital resources and a higher output transcending the increase of population and, therefore, with a higher standard of living. The question is whether immigration is the total answer or merely coincidental. Immigration can certainly offer a way out of certain economic maladjustments and can be salutary and stimulating for the economic development of the country, but only if linked with capital import permitting a better use of resources and higher production.

Economic growth in Israel rests, then, on an economy of growing population, which is conducive to the enlargement of productive capacity. As early as the end of the eighteenth century, Joseph von Sonnenfels described the rationale:

> Ten people have ten requirements. The requirements of
> one create employment, income and means of subsistence
> for the others. In this way 10 men create 10 sources of
> income for 10 others. 10 additional people would have 10
> more requirements, but would bring with them at the same
> time 10 additional sources of income.[1]

Another writer of that age, Jakob Friedrich von Bielfeld, likewise
concludes:

> If one were to fill an uninhabited country with animals they
> would soon consume all food and pasture. If on the other
> hand an uninhabited country were filled with people, there
> would soon be an excess of the necessities of life. It is
> incredible how much help one man gets from the other.[2]

The mechanism of economy of a growing population was the
driving force behind the movements of colonization in the eighteenth
and nineteenth centuries. But currently, as indicated, to embark in
a new country upon the production of primary commodities for export,
as in the early phase of colonization, becomes profitable only under
exceptionally favorable conditions since world markets are burdened
with the dead weight of surplus stocks of almost every such commodity.

A steady level of production and contracting markets for primary
products impose constraints on the structural growth of developing
countries which, on that account, have deflected their efforts toward
a diversification of their economies by putting more emphasis on
secondary industries. They are in the course of being industrialized
and of superimposing, on their economic foundations, the strata of
secondary and tertiary occupations.

However, the economic growth of Israel is a different phenom-
onon that calls for explanation and analysis in the light of general
world trends and developments. Israel is not a colonization venture
of traditional pattern but rather a transplantation of population, a
transplantation that took place in the form of a transfer, in sudden
tides, of immigrants possessing the prerequisites of skill and capital
and automatically providing their own internal market. It presupposes
an artificial noneconomic propulsion, a rapid movement of people
telescoped into a short space of time.

Immigration into Israel is not the result of a population readjustment effected by a transfer from areas of intenser to areas
of lighter pressure on economic resources. It is powered by a dynamo of political and extra-economic forces, as noted by Macpherson:

It should be recalled, for instance, that the reason for
many of the migrations that are taking place today is
racial and not economic, and that, in fact, a great many
people are moving from country to country not because
they wish to better their standards of living, but because
they happen to belong to a race which is not wanted in the
country from which they move away. In that connection,
I would remind you of what is in my opinion one of the
most interesting examples of the problems of racial redistribution, but one which has not so far been referred to:
the problem of the movement of the Jews to Palestine. If
we are going to attempt to be realistic, it seems to me
that we should at least remember that such migration is
going on, and not refer to the colonial and economic aspects of the problem alone to the exclusion of those which
are purely national and essentially racial. [3]

The interaction of dynamic factors working upon the economy
of Israel as a receptacle of transplantation accentuated the fluctuations
in all economic indexes beyond the usual swings due to import of
capital and manpower. The balance of trade is highly adverse. The
section of the economy that is based on new investment is large in
comparison with the established base and, projected onto the economic
structure, immensely influences economic fluctuations and widens
the range of economic expansion and contraction. It is development
by undulation with the peak of each wave overtopping its forerunners.
These mechanics are not altogether unlike what was common in
countries of colonization in the nineteenth century. In Canada, New
Zealand, Australia, and Argentina, one may discern alternating
phases of high immigration, which coincide with booms, and of low
immigration, coinciding with crises. Generally speaking, each
succeeding cycle of immigration attained a higher level than the one
before it as the new economy broadened its base and became capable
of absorbing a greater number of newcomers.

The a priori theoretical assumption that immigration, expansion
of production and consumption, and access of capital are interdependent
is corroborated by quantitative and statistical tests (see Chapter 5).

A summary of the evidence available so far warrants the conclusion that Israel is a country of rapid economic growth into which
a new population is being rapidly transplanted and where high imports
and an adverse trade balance are the inevitable concomitants. As
long as a copious and constant stream of immigration is being absorbed
and new farms and factories are being established, home production,
whether of consumption or capital goods, must lag behind the needs

of the growing population. The adverse trade balance in itself is
not a sign of economic disequilibrium; it is only to be expected that,
in the circumstances of Israel, for some time production will fail
to keep pace with the demands of an ever increasing population. If
the gap between imports and exports is bridged by influx of capital,
the consequent cessation of capital imports will lessen the volume
of imports and the adverse trade balance will of necessity adjust
itself, investment will dwindle, and fewer capital goods be brought
in; the import surplus will be diminished and the natural process of
fruition of the heavy capital imports of earlier years is bound to step
up local production and reduce dependence on foreign supplies. Investments are maturing and their maturity means larger exports,
whereas the import of consumers' goods per capita will be reduced.
Export statistics offer a further test of this truth. On the other hand,
rising imports of industrial machinery reflect industrialization and
imports of farm machinery reflect the modernization of agriculture.

The full employment prevailing in Israel in periods when immigration is extensive is always linked with a concurrent high level of
investment. The curve of employment climbs steadily after a rise
in immigration and in sympathy with expansion of productive forces
while the curve of unemployment is traced in inverse ratio: apart
from slight deviations due to time lags, crests of immigration coincide with troughs of unemployment and contrariwise, with the sole
exception of the first three years after the establishment of the state
when population doubled. That unemployment did not go up for all
the increment of new arrivals is a very practical confirmation of the
theoretical case against the "lump of labor" thesis. * It is a fact
recognized by the man in the street, who stoutly believes that "immigration creates work, " an empricial conclusion that conforms well
with that reached by the reasoning of the economist. R. F. Harrod
states:

> The notion that the existence of unemployment is a good
> reason for discouraging immigration appears wholly
> fallacious. Each extra resident is a consumer as well
> as a producer. . . . The notion that a bare reduction
> of the number of residents would serve to reduce the
> number of unemployed, and an increase to increase

————————————

*"Lump of labor" theory assumes a constant volume of em-
ployment in a given area; if population and labor force increase unemployment must result. This theory disregards changes arising
out of growth of population or consumption, new skills, initiatives,
etc.

unemployment, has always been regarded as crude in the
extreme by those who have given any thought to the problem involved. [4]

The fallacy of the "lump of labor" thesis is also attacked by H. D.
Henderson:

> It is supposed that the amount of employment available
> in any country at a given time is independent of the
> number of persons in that country. This, however, is
> not the case. Every individual is a consumer as well
> as a producer. He helps to give employment to others
> as well as helping to increase the supply of labor. It
> is, indeed, impossible to determine whether the ad-
> mission of immigrants is more likely in general to
> increase or to diminish unemployment. The answer
> must depend partly upon the particular industrial apti-
> tude of the immigrants and partly on the economic cir-
> cumstances prevailing at the time in the country to
> which they go. [5]

Both these rebuttals of a widespread economic fallacy are based
on theoretical inference. The Israel experiment is a classic and
successful check, practical and empirical, of their validity. Here,
as far as it goes, experience upholds deduction. The transformation
of Israel's economy by the very process of comigration (immigration
linked with import of capital), the expansion of markets, and the
ensuing expansion of production all go to show how immigration
creates its own absorptive capacity, how economic conditions may
become a function of the process of migration.

Apparently, not the quantitative volume of labor but the relative
proportion of labor to economic factors determines the degree of
employment or unemployment. When immigration and capital are
pouring in, most of the attendant expansion is in the investment
sector of the economy. In a period of contraction, labor is set free
by a halt in new investment but is gradually reabsorbed by the agricultural and industrial enterprises founded by previous investment
and now producing. A sediment of unemployed is left but, under the
special conditions of an economy of transplantation, it is smaller in
a broad-based than it would be in a narrow economy. The larger
the economy, the less, again relatively, the importance of immigration and new investments and the easier the absorption of labor
that was previously employed on the investment sector. The progress
of economic enterprises depends a great deal on market opportunities
and, since almost every branch of production requires a certain
technical minimum of demand for its sound economic establishment,

the bigger the population the larger the section of the economy that
can be run viably and the simpler it is to absorb any manpower laid
off by curtailment or stoppage of new investment.

In other words, labor is absorbed by the maturing of investments made during a period of expansion. In the pre-state period,
each contraction after a spell of expansion led to a slump but equilibrium was reestablished fairly soon in what was even then defined as
a "plastic and resilient" economy:

> Palestine has had a series of disturbances since 1920 and
> has shown that its economic structure is both plastic and
> resilient; plastic because Jews decline to permit economic
> catastrophe in the country in which their National Home
> is permitted; resilient because both the Arabs and the
> Jews insist on continuing to live as such. [6]

After a period of contraction, the expansion that ensues, starting
as it does from the new point of departure, is always greater: the
economy is propped up not only by the wider scope of production
due to more demand but also by its diversified character, mirrored
in a changing occupational distribution of labor. In Israel's first
years of statehood, its financial, employment, and trade statistics
pointed in a single direction. An expansion means an adverse trade
balance, which goes hand in hand with import of capital, greater
consumption of goods, and more investment. The imported capital
serves mainly to expand the economy and for new investment; if it
contracts, the excess of imports over exports also contracts. Analysis
of trade in physical and money terms is corroborative of these sub-
missions. Employment attests a particular mechanism of readjustment to economic setbacks: labor employed in the investment economy,
particularly in building activity, is laid off, only to be speedily taken
on again in undertakings established in the period of contraction, and
the percentage of unemployment drops in direct ratio to the broadening
of the economic base.

These underlying trends are soundly diagnosed and analyzed
in the following excerpt from a report issued in 1931 by the British
Mandatory Administration of Palestine:

> Natural increases and migration bear upon the movement
> of the population; economic circumstances, determined
> by the whole world, bear upon the subsistence available
> and control, in some way imperfectly understood, both
> migration and natural increase; and finally, both migration
> and natural increase influence economic circumstances
> within Palestine itself. In a comparatively small

population, inhabiting a country lacking obvious natural
resources, migration is an important factor. It can
operate on the population by the actual addition or with-
drawal of persons; by changing the age composition of
the population, it can alter its fertility; and, in relation
to general economic conditions, it can better or worsen
the conditions favorable to the rate of increase of the
total population. Of the past history of migration it is
true to say that, as human intelligence and industry came
into play, the means of livelihood have been extended,
and hence as population has multiplied, the production
of material subsistence has increased. . . .

Undoubtedly, the annual increase of subsistence so
far has been due to the policy of immigration. Immigration has not only stimulated local production and so enabled
the sale of Palestine produce abroad, but has introduced
invisible import of value into the country and so raised
capacity to purchase its requirements where these are
not satisfied by internal production. [7]

A balance set under such conditions is the dynamic equilibrium of an
economy of expansion geared to impulses of extraneous extra-economic
forces that give rise to cycles of development with each broader-
based than its predecessor.

Harry Jerome's investigation into migration and business
cycles finds a very near concurrence of the two. As far as the United
States is concerned, in almost every case prosperity was simultaneous
in the country of emigration and in the country of absorption and led
to greater immigration. But Jerome admits that "There are a number
of instances, particularly at the turning points of moderate booms
or depressions, where the immigration curve turns first. "[8]

The point is also made by other investigators in a wider context.
"Men do not emigrate in despair but in hope, " say researchers of
migration movements. As to the position in the United States, Germany, and Great Britain, Hanson concludes that the cycles do run
together. However, Jerome and others make allowance for exceptional
eventualities when the repelling forces are the mainspring of migration:
Jerome gives the instances of potato famines in Ireland and the disaster
that befell Armenia in 1920. But usually large migrations are contemporaneous with prosperity in the countries both of departure and
of destination.

Israel is nonconformist here, resembling rather the exceptions
of Ireland and Armenia. Plainly, a small country like Israel, with

its unique quantitative and qualitative interrelationship of immigrants
and established inhabitants, must stray from Jerome's norm.   That
very interrelationship reverses the process described by him.   The
powerful swing of the migration pendulum and the fluctuations that
it provokes are too violent to permit a stereotyped internal business
cycle to develop, although they can influence almost every other
reverberation of economic life.

In considering the effect of migration on the business cycle,
Jerome mentions the following probability:

> The inflow of large numbers of new workers into the
> United States in times of prosperity has been a factor
> in increasing the intensity of boom periods and con-
> sequently the severity of the subsequent depression. . . .
> Although a decline in employment is usually followed
> by a decline in immigration, the incoming stream does
> not dry up entirely, and in those portions of de-
> pression periods in which there is a net immigration—
> a not uncommon phenomenon—migration is feeding into
> industry more men than it is taking out. [9]

To confine the analysis of the influence of migration on a country's economy to the factor of employment, labor supply and wages
may be appropriate whenever immigration stands in such a ratio
to existing population as renders its impact unimpressive both numerically and by reason, as a rule, of its lower standard and inferior
economic value.   The situation is entirely different in Israel, where
the new influx decisively influences economic conditions.   Large-
scale immigration is followed by sudden expansion of demand, introduction of capital and its diffusion through building channels, qualitative shifts in consumption and structural changes in markets, a
stimulus to install an apparatus of production relying on new marketing
prospects and, in short, an economy galvanized into growth.   Here
Jerome's thesis that immigration is a function of the economic conditions of the country of absorption is turned upside down: those conditions become a function of immigration.

In Israel, as noted, building and public works were a natural
outcome of the entry of capital and manpower side by side.   The
building industry sparked off a general process of development, tided
newcomers over their settling-in period, and was a lever of all other
forms of enterprise, effects that, already in Mandate times, fully
warranted the opinion that the demand for labor in the construction
industry or the development of the infrastructure served to accelerate
economic growth and to some extent iron out the fluctuations of the
business cycle.

The interplay of these factors is bound up with effective demand since it generates sufficient purchasing power to absorb the flow of commodities from factory and field. That consumption has not lagged behind production goes a long way toward explaining Israel's rapid development. Effective demand suffices to draw new industries to what would otherwise be considered the most unlikely areas. The capital imported and locally available was ready to grasp any opportunity for investment if only a market could be found. The stream of immigration assured the market, and capital was invested forthwith in the production necessary to meet the bigger demand. This new production concentrated on the domestic market.

It becomes clear that immigration itself, so viewed, has accelerated development. If the immigrants had held back until the new factories were put up and come in only then, in all probability development would have been brought to a standstill. The plants would never have gone up until a market for their output was guaranteed, thus starting a vicious circle. Only with the arrival of immigrants with effective purchasing power imported at the same time from public and private sources did production expand to meet the newcomers' requirements. Again the paradox: it is easier for an economy to absorb more than fewer immigrants, and sudden and swift absorption is more successful than slow and gradual infiltration. For a trickle of immigrants, infiltration is not enough to provide a sufficient home market, whereas a numerous inflow affords the opportunity for profitable large-scale production so long as the import of capital pari passu matches the inflow and is adjusted to it:

> Population, indeed, affects the optimum output not only directly, inasmuch as it is a factor of production, but also indirectly by the extent of consumption of the entire population, active and inactive (young and old, sick people and other dependants). . . . Division of labor causes expansion of the market, so that the demand for certain goods becomes large enough to ensure a livelihood for a certain number of individuals. [10]

Of course, this expansion is always conditioned by a country's natural limitations but, as the modes of modern production and technology develop, these have less and less influence:

> In the decades immediately preceding the War, and still more in the first post-war decade, the relatively more rapid rate of increase of consumer's demand in North and South America, Australia and New Zealand has provided a powerful incentive to localization of manufacturing industries in those regions, and the same forces are observable also in Asia. [11]

The import of capital cannot of itself trigger off an investment boom of the kind that took place in Israel: only an amalgam of accumulated capital and the rising and reinforced demand that new immigration engenders could start the economic onset, and that onset could be kept going only by virtue of the peculiar make-up of the investment, which at first concerned itself chiefly with building and then with expanding production for a home market that had thus come into being. Admittedly, this sequence of reinforcement of demand by new immigration, building, and capital import has its limits. In a period of structural development, "full employment" can be achieved and pegged for a considerable length of time. But when that period runs out, a gap must appear between growth of production and growth of purchasing power, and the temporary bridging of the gap, although it brings prosperity, cannot permanently resolve the basic long-term problems of the economy. On the other hand, it has played its part as an instrument of dynamic expansion and bequeaths a broader-based and more sophisticated economy.

For the peculiarity that noneconomic factors gave birth to the conditions for the rapid growth of Israel's economy there is a precedent in the general experience of other countries where rearmament on the eve of hostilities quickly cut down unemployment. "Full employment" necessarily presupposes a certain volume of investment. In Israel, the inducement to invest is provided by the import of purchasing power and a countrywide diffusion of capital that spans the disparity between production and purchasing power: mass immigration, with simultaneous import of capital, gives extra-economic impulsion to the development of a new economy, and the wheels of that economy start turning.

The activating reciprocity between the economy of Israel and the human inflow that the country tapped and that itself set new economic forces in motion was the hallmark of this transplantation. In a little more than two decades, Israel absorbed 1.2 million immigrants with the net increment constituting 37 percent of the population. With immigration came a capital import of $10 billion. Not only did real gross production per capita rise by 210 percent between 1950 and 1970 but also the standard of living improved notably, as witnessed by a rise of some 145 percent in the real consumption of goods and services per capita.

Unusual economic conditions have made the functional interdependence of immigration and absorptive capacity more pronounced in Israel than elsewhere. Israel's high ratio of immigrants to settled population, of rare occurrence as it is in the history of migration, has been further emphasized by the heavier specific economic weight of the immigrants and has wrought radical changes in the economy.

The salient stages of the development are the impact of a highly modernized Western system on an embryonic economy, the transformation of that embryo into a semi-industrialized organism, the superimposition of that organism on what preexisted, and the graudal transition from a subsistence to an exchange economy. The intenser migration to Israel in a period when migratory movements were generally slowing down, the size of the migration by comparison with the existing population, the divergences and deviations in quantity and quality from world trends—these are the background to the process of Israel's economic growth.

NOTES

1. See Joseph von Sonnenfels, Handbuch der Staatsverwaltung, (Vienna, 1798), pp. 110ff.; See Paul Mombert, "Wirtschaft und Bevolkerung," in Grundiss der Sozialokonomik, II (Tubingen: Verlag I. C. B. Mohr, 1914), p. 68.

2. Mombert, op. cit.; von Bielfeld, Lehrbegriff der Staatskunst, (Breslau, 1761) p. 118.

3. Macpherson, "The Colonial Question, Raw Materials and Markets", in Peaceful Change, Procedures, Population Pressure, (Paris: League of Nations, 1938), p. 392.

4. R. F. Harrod in the Manchester Guardian, July 12, 1938. Cited in D. F. Buxton, The Economics of the Refugee Problem, (London: Focus Publishing Co. Ltd., 1938), pp. 12, 13.

5. Sir John Hope Simpson, The Refugee Problem, Report of a Survey, (London: Oxford University Press for Royal Institute of International Affairs, 1939), p. 606.

6. Government of Palestine, Department of Migration, Annual Report, 1936, p. 21.

7. Government of Palestine, Census of Palestine, 1931, Vol. I, Part 1, pp. 46-47.

8. Harry Jerome, Migration and Business Cycles (New York: National Bureau of Economic Research, New York, 1926), p. 242.

9. Ibid., p. 242.

10. Imre Ferenczi, The Synthetic Optimum of Population, (Paris: League of Nations, 1938), p. 46.

11. League of Nations, World Economic Survey, 1931/32 (Geneva), p. 18.

INTRODUCTION TO PART II

The process of transplantation, as reflected in the analysis of its mechanism and driving forces, had precedents in the colonization of new countries overseas, particularly in the British Dominions in the eighteenth and nineteenth centuries, but Israel's economic growth exhibits distinctive features. These are the rise in population and GNP in relation to the base from which the rise started, the telescoping of the process into a short space of time, a background of particularly adverse conditions such as scarcity of natural resources and a precarious security due to geopolitical conditions, extra-economic motivations, the absence of factors of economic gravitation that would add to the country's attraction for large-scale immigration and import of capital, and the timing of the process when the transplantations that had been of such frequent occurrence in the nineteenth century had, for the most part, virtually come to an end.

Transplantation on the largest scale, namely, in the first years of the Israeli state, was determined in the main by exogenous forces and factors of immigration and transfer of capital. The basis for future developments was laid down on these first elements of growth, but they were not exclusive and to some extent tapered off, particularly as the weight of the exogenous forces and factors fell with the self-expansion of the autonomous body economic that they had formed and furthered. In this subsequent period, internal economic forces and factors gained in importance. Structural changes in the young body economic, and economic policies, wielded an influence that became increasingly pronounced. The quantitative ratio between the exogenous and the immanent in the economy was substantially altered, involving a gradual deflection of impact from the former to the latter. These alterations, such as the shift in weight from agriculture to industry, the diminishing weight of staple industries (e.g., textile and food processing) and the heavier weight of more sophisticated industries, the more marked export orientation of the economy, and the rise in productivity as a significant factor in economic growth are analyzed in greater detail in Part II.

Economic policy exerts a formidable influence on economic growth and development. Thus, in the period that followed rapid demographic expansion after the establishment of the state, a lessening of the weight of exogenous factors added moment to structural changes in the economy itself and to economic policies that call for explanation as they take greater effect, against the background of economic expansion in the preceding period of accelerated growth. Exogenous factors still interacted with internal elements, immigration continued even if at a slower rate, and import of capital was especially significant in advancing economic growth and in connection with the problem of the overall balance of payments.

In the circumstances, the main policy objective, the main problem confronting the government, was the "trade-off" of economic growth and inflation. To what extent could inflation be countenanced under conditions of rapid economic growth? How far should effective and excessive demand be checked, considering its encouragement of that growth at least in the initial period? How was it possible to reconcile acquiescence in excessive demand as a growth-stimulant with attainment of the economic independence that had to be achieved in the long run because of constraints in the balance of payments accentuated by the prospect of a petering out of unilateral transfers and of an intolerable burden of external debt?

Obviously, it became essential to use all instruments of economic policy-fiscal, monetary, and incomes-to withstand inflationary pressures and balance contradictory factors, to prevent stagnation and runaway inflation alike. Each policy ran into trouble, its effectiveness impaired by internal polarities. Such fiscal measures as high taxation encountered limitations inevitably set by the need to step up productivity per man-hour; monetary policy was hamstrung by the need to finance expanding production and attract large-scale investment; control of rising incomes was neutralized to some extent by the policy of full employment; the erosion of money values undermined thrift. Yet for most of the time there was an overwhelming necessity to integrate a backlog of unabsorbed newcomers and new immigrants.

Thus, there were built-in irreconcilables in Israel's economic policy: absorption of immigration requiring swift economic growth as against the goal of economic independence, which meant a drastic change in the balance of payments if the excess of imports over exports was to be cut down, which depended partly on the stability of prices and incomes that is indispensable for expansion of export but would hardly be consistent with overheated economic activity and overfull employment. In this predicament, economic policy vacillated frequently and unorthodox methods were employed to meet emergencies and surmount difficulties. High customs tariffs made for a substitution of imports by local production but affected Israel's competitive capacity on export markets; export premiums led to distortions in fiscal policy and price pattern; considerations of the balance of payments could not be harmonized with the aim of speeding economic growth at almost any price.

This extraordinary situation could not be tackled without widening the scope of official intervention and giving government activity a greater weight within the economy, with the consequence that the free interplay of economic forces was often displaced by administrative

controls, sometimes with unfortunate results, manifest in particular
in strong and virtually unremitting inflationary pressures; warped
patterns of production, prices, and trade; and some misallocation and
waste of resources.

Only once, and then briefly, in the years 1965-66 did the divergent
and conflicting alternatives compel economic policy to abandon its
preference for rapid economic growth over a greater measure of
balance and stability. The controversy as to whether this departure
reflected deliberate policy or the impact of recessionary forces, or
a combination of the two in varying doses, has never been settled. In
those two years, unemployment rose from 3.6 to 7.4 percent of the
labor force, the rise in incomes was checked, the balance of payments
improved considerably, and the excess of imports over exports de-
creased. But this recession meant much misery, however assuaged
by governmental measures of social aid, and it also meant stagnation
in economic growth, a fall in immigration figures, and even some
emigration. However, this situation was radically changed by the Six-
Day War of 1967 and the war economy.

The rapid economic growth generated in the boom periods of
immigration and the war economy produced more openings for employment than could be filled by the larger labor force, and the ensuing
pressures led to higher incomes on a national scale and per man-hour
as well because of the insistent pressures for higher wages that overfull employment induced. Import of capital exceeding the excess of
imports over exports led to overinvestment, overliquidity, and overconsumption. Currency surpluses monetized by conversion into local
currency built up inflationary thrusts that raised prices and enlarged
the excess of imports over exports. In sum, there was hectic economic activity on the one hand with distortions of pattern and misallocation of resources on the other.

Furthermore, the countercyclical policy of the government, aiming
at a blend of stability and rapid economic growth, met with formidable
political and social resistance that can be ascribed to economic conditions and to an inordinate and precipitate rise in standards of living,
and was compounded by large security expenditure.

It is possible under these circumstances to draw up a balance-
sheet of economic policy. Obviously, the results cannot be unequi-
vocal. It is true that inflationary pressures could not be sufficiently
contained, but economic growth was accelerated at unprecedented speed.
Too many objectives were pursued at the same time: security, integration of newcomers and progress in social welfare, and, simultaneously, a spectacular rise in general standards of living and consumption. The disparity between expansion of incomes, supply of money

and credit, and real resources was patent practically throughout, with repercussions on price levels and the balance of payments, the two interchanging in various degrees at different times. Immigration and large-scale investment were the main destabilizing factors but also were the chief agents and stimulants of rapid economic growth.

Yet despite all this inner array of contradictory forces, no little progress was registered: demographic expansion which for noneconomic reasons became a target of economic policy, the integration since the establishment of the state of nearly 1.25 million newcomers, massive investment, reinforcement of security, higher standards of living and social welfare, a fair measure of social and political internal stability, and avoidance of runaway inflation.

True, the cost was heavy in terms of resources, instability, and distortions in the economic pattern, but in the final verdict it must be borne in mind that the aims went far beyond exclusively economic considerations and there is no mistaking their substantial fulfillment.

THE TARGETS AND INGREDIENTS OF
ECONOMIC POLICY IN ISRAEL

A growth policy presupposes a purposive economy aiming at definite tasks and targets. To be effective, it must be shaped to the mold of local economic conditions and the political and social setting of its society.

There is a general consensus as to objectives in Israel: continuous large-scale immigration and integration of immigrants in the country's socioeconomic fabric, economic independence, avoidance of major unemployment, and a more efficient use of resources; these noncontroversial objectives complement one another.

Foreign trade necessarily occupies a central position in solving the problem of a small country with scarce natural resources: in the smaller of the developed countries of Europe, exports absorb as much as 30 to 40 percent of the GNP. The same applies to the question of full employment. With the end of the boom that first follows immigration, import of capital, and expansion of effective demand, export industries become the most welcome and natural sources of employment in Israel. They should also supply the foreign currency needed to buy the commodities that cannot be economically produced at home, the bulk of which represent such components of production as capital goods, fuel, raw materials, and spare parts. In Israel, artificial employment by way of inflated building or production predominantly for the home market to satisfy excessive demand is possible only if capital is imported or if reserves of foreign currency are depleted and an already onerous indebtedness is augmented.

Therefore, the threads in the wide tapestry of Israel's economic policy may be woven together in a simple sentence: the intent has been to telescope within two decades an economic growth that should normally take half a century.

Manifold troubles and contradictions are involved. The policy must ensure a rapid rise in the GNP so that local production can be substituted for an import of capital that may dwindle in the not too distant future. And this development must occur under conditions of full employment and be dovetailed with the integration of immigrants. To accomplish this goal without falling into the trap of an inflation that would defeat the whole purpose of the exercise is difficult, dangerous, and full of inner contradictions.

The economic forecast assumes that net import of capital will taper off gradually with the disappearance of personal restitution and a decrease in loans and that at the same time, substantially larger amounts will be needed for the state's debt service. Only swift development could lead to a decrease in the deficit in the balance of payments that a dwindling import of capital and a more costly servicing of state indebtedness must entail. Consequently, it is essential to expand productive capacity and provide a livelihood for a population that has multiplied more than threefold within the years 1948-71. This is a two-pronged undertaking: to transform the economy of the state and to transform its growing population. Here is the heart of Israel's economic and social problems.

Under existing circumstances, the dual metamorphosis calls for extensive exploitation of such natural resources as are available, with the help of imported capital and the accumulation of capital and savings at home. Investment must not involve capital alone; simultaneously, skills, prospecting and exploration, research and knowhow, and foreign trade must play a central part.

But the preconditions of an effective economic policy are lacking in Israel, where exogenous factors and forces are overwhelmingly preponderant. Countercyclical policies are frustrated by sharp fluctuations in import of capital and immigration. The internal sequence of boom and recession is overborne and pales into insignificance if the distance between the autonomy of indigenous factors and external economic forces is as wide as it is here.

Moreover, the multiplicity and diversity of tasks, some of them at first sight beyond performance, are serious handicaps to the effectiveness of economic policy. Proportionately the heaviest defense budget in the world, a population that more than trebled within two decades, a rise of 145 percent in the standard of living, the absorption of 1.2 million immigrants of a hundred origins, a far-ranging occupational reshuffle, a structural remodeling of the economy, and an unparalleled sevenfold real rise in GNP—these are bound to signify an expansion that strains resources tremendously. In short, conscious policy in Israel is endeavoring to gain too many simultaneous objectives with limited means and certain distortions and failures, particularly inflation, are inescapable in the circumstances.

On the other hand, the reaction to the magnitude of the task, the response to the vast challenge, called compellingly for variety and flexibility in economic policy: it had to be pragmatic, unorthodox, and experimental with neither tradition nor dogma shackling it.

In the application of a conglomerate of measures of economic policy, a strong bias toward expansion was evident: steps to accelerate development were widely preferred to any that tended to retard over-expansion, and a swifter tempo of growth took priority over any braking or curbing of excessive and overheated activity.

The OECD Observer of June 1970 defines the "major policy problem" of the organization's member states as follows:

To ensure an adequate and stable growth of demand so that the potential growth of output is fully realised without endangering internal or external stability:

-to achieve a better direction of the growth process so that the extra wealth is used to meet the needs and wants of society and the damaging side effects of growth are prevented.

The assurance of a satisfying and stable growth of demand was self-implementing in Israel, determined by exogenous factors; thus, economic policy should have aimed at the other targets in the main. Actually, however, policy did not always accept these facts and conditions and concentrated almost uninterruptedly, with the sole exception of the years 1965-66, on accelerating and stimulating economic activity. The upshot was strong labor-market pressures, rapid price rises, and deficits in the balance of payments.

This does not mean that stagnation and unemployment were never experienced. They resulted from bottlenecks in the economy, fluctuations in capital import, maladjustment and discrepancies between import of capital and import of manpower, whose crests and troughs did not always coincide, but they were always shortlived and overcompensated by subsequent spells of expansion and growth, except in the two years 1965-66.

With encouragement of investment the first and foremost objective, the following actions were taken:

1. A law for the encouragement of capital investments made
provision for direct government grants and long-term loans on concessionary terms, particularly to be invested in export-oriented
branches and in enterprises in "development areas" in agriculture,
industry, and transport in order to facilitate the dispersal of population
in the light of defense considerations and the concern with ecological
problems.

2. The government engaged directly in establishing the infrastructure required for an expanding economy, in transport and communications and so forth.

3. With some help from private, public, and semipublic financing,
the government assumed a major responsibility in financing applied
research and development, establishing and maintaining institutions
of higher learning, and making training facilities available to youth
and immigrant labor.

4. The government was prominent in furnishing homes for the
rapidly growing population, and particularly for immigrants, on concessionary and sometimes even nominal terms.

5. Subsidies were granted to infant industries and for export
promotion and foreign market research.

6. New farm villages were fully and continuously financed by
government and the Jewish Agency, until each became self-supporting.

7. In the underwriting of this multitude of diversified projects
all designed to hasten economic growth, new, imaginative, and original
measures were boldly and extensively adopted.

8. The sizable development budgets of government and the
Jewish Agency were financed by Diaspora gift funds, West German
reparations, credits from international institutions, long-term issue
of government bonds at home and overseas, and borrowings from
foreign banks, particularly in the United States.

9. The local capital market was monopolized by the state and
a part of the funds raised there was used for the same development
budgets in directions and for purposes fixed by government policy.

10. In 1952, the government began to issue real-value guaranteed
bonds linked to the dollar (until 1962) or the cost-of-living index
(throughout). This method of financing had a multiple purpose: to
raise funds for development, to narrow government budgetary deficits
in periods of inflation, and to encourage savings and accumulation of

capital in periods of unstable prices and erosion of local currency values.

11. Quantitative and qualitative controls of credit, the first in restriction and containment of inflationary pressures, the second for channeling and earmarking financial resources for priority economic development, were largely used. Both ends were met by prescribing and varying reserve requirements, which always were put higher than was necessary and desirable for anti-inflationary purposes, and a proportion of the resultant deposits were reserved to encourage priority production by exemptions accorded within quantified limits. It was, indeed, a method of combining selective credit policy with anti-inflationary action.

12. Compulsory loans were imposed parallel to heavy taxation and the burden shouldered by all strata of Israel's society was made that much heavier.

Thus, with all external factors growth- and expansion-oriented, the principal shortcoming of economic policy was a failure to use restrictive devices more frequently and with greater vigor although, as may be seen from the foregoing catalog of measures taken, such devices were part and parcel of economic policy. The emphasis was almost always on physical expansion and not enough was done to halt the growth of demand. Restraints, if and when applied, were reversed too hurriedly.

Perfect harmonization of economic policy with economic needs could hardly be expected, particularly under conditions such as those prevailing in Israel with so many objectives beyond the reach of material resources: security, development, welfare, and the struggle against poverty. The OECD comments on this problem as follows:

> Experience suggests that perfectly steady rates of increase
> in aggregate demand and output are an unattainable ideal.
> There will always be mistakes in diagnosing the situation,
> errors of forecasting and miscalculations about the precise
> effects of a particular set of policy measures on the pattern
> of economic development. Moreover, given the political
> and institutional obstacles to rapid action in this field,
> there will always be problems posed by the reaction time
> of the authorities.[1]

In Israel, an overheated economic activity made for a rise in monetary and real incomes so that prices rose and the balance of payments deteriorated. Surplus liquidity, overemployment, and an expansion of projects of investment exceeding real resources partly neutralized efforts to conduct a countercyclical policy of restraint.

The fallacy that expansion of production will of itself bring enough real resources into being to balance the higher incomes and consumption has found wide public acceptance and support, in disregard of the corollary truth that inflationary pressures are the concomitant of the additional incomes that expanded production generates. To master these trends and developments in the economy, the government was obliged to take firm restrictive and countercyclical steps including forced loans, issue of dollar- and index-linked securities, quantitative and qualitative credit controls, open-market operations, severe taxation and cuts in budgetary expenditures. Yet the economic policy had inherent contradictions since it called for more investment to redress the current balance of payments and find employment for newcomers. This demanded the mobilization of funds abroad with the consequence of a monetization of surpluses in the overall balance, and the next phase was monetary expansion and inflation.

Nevertheless, the policy was not altogether unsuccessful in speeding economic growth without starting a self-perpetuating runaway inflation although, naturally, under unprecedented pressures of the magnitude experienced by Israel, some disregard of a desirable order of priorities, some overlooking of alternative uses of resources in every investment or economic project was not uncommon. Monetization of surpluses in the overall balance of payments during almost the entire period until 1968 intensified inflationary pressures. Economic criteria were not applied adequately in the use of resources and the promotion of enterprises. Wrong priorities and errors of judgment in investment could hardly be avoided. The tactics of incentives and disincentives in economic policy as practiced by a highly centralized authority could not always be properly integrated into the pattern of macro-economic design.

Endeavors to draw nearer to the economic independence that was the supreme objective were set at naught more than once by external events exploding in conflict and war. Such events meant unproductive use of resources. Internal social pressures, particularly under conditions of boom and overfull employment most of the time, frequently defeated government policies intended to slow down an excessive growth of private consumption.

Economic policy endeavored to activate countervailing forces that would help to overcome the contradictions inherent in rapid economic growth. The line of policy that limits fluctuations yet averts deflationary crises, inflationary prosperity, and a swollen local demand is not the easiest to pursue, especially in a modern economy. A. H. Hansen wrote:

In our modern, highly complicated economic order, we are continually in danger. It is not easy to keep the system in balance. We are compelled to keep our hand on the throttle in order to ensure an adequate, but not excessive, aggregate demand.

A more sophisticated direction of economic growth might have yielded more of the extra resources that were needed to satisfy the multifarious claims upon limited resources. Yet continuity of rapid economic growth contributed to some extent to satisfying these claims. The important thing was to instill the recognition that at any given time it is impossible to do everything at once. Israel's "brains trusts" have been grappling interminably with this dilemma and setting about the choice of priorities with courage and commendable ingenuity, reflected for example in the use of unpopular currency measures of currency readjustment in no less than six devaluations in 1949, 1952, 1953, 1962, 1967 and 1971, some overdue but all helpful in restoring, by flexibility to exchange, some equilibrium to the economy.

Overcentralization and too much dependence on individual decisions, lack of consistency in policy, and a neglect of criteria have occasionally wrecked otherwise resourceful and pliable economic strategies. The polymorphic climate of the economy unquestionably fertilized new sources of enterprise, but it also complicated the tasks of the policy-makers.

The self-defeating character of excessively rising money incomes gave the government no option but to buttress its fiscal and monetary defenses by an incomes policy, a step that was rendered a little easier by a personal nexus of the cabinet ministers and the trade union leadership within the same political framework: temporary freezes of wages and prices were enforced, but never by statutory enactment.

Commenting on the readiness of the trade unions to help in carrying out a reasonable incomes policy, a very important international financial institution, basing itself on expert investigations, had this to say:

> The prospects for implementing an incomes policy appear more favorable in Israel than in most other countries. The attitude expressed by the Histadrut to us is that wages should be determined in the light of the needs of the overall economy for sustained growth with stability rather than on the basis of narrow interests, a much more responsible attitude than that shown by representatives of workers of other countries. This is, perhaps, to be regarded as a measure of the national solidarity of Israel.

In Israel, the efforts to match rapid economic growth with stability encountered all the usual setbacks, but with the exacerbations

and aggravations that geopolitical, demographic, and social pressures
bring about. This exceptional conjunction necessitated a diversity of
highly unorthodox, pragmatic, daring, and innovative policies that
had more than one spectacular success but could not altogether escape
failings in the use and direction of resources or economic maladjustments and imbalances. Rapid economic growth, overfull employment,
an immense import of capital, a high level of investment, and the
government's monetary expansion because of large expenditure on defense and on economic development built up powerful inflationary pressures. In the end, a confrontation could not be avoided between the
urgency of rapid economic growth, an urgency of objective warrant,
and the need to hold in those pressures. This was one of the crucial
problems inseparable from the circumstances, and mainly an issue
of policy.

In the long run, rapid economic growth is predicated on a control
of inflation, as is attested by the experience of Indonesia and certain
Latin American states. At first inflation will stimulate the growth,
but if the inflationary process is continuous and swift the resulting
distortions make for erosion of money, elimination of most criteria
of sound investment, balance of payments difficulties, and, consequently, a shortage of foreign currency and a rise in prices which
initiate a second round of inflationary expectations—a self-propelling
spiral that it is difficult to stop. This happened in Israel also, markedly in the first years of the state.

For Israel, however, the cyclical fluctuations are of fairly
circumscribed influence. Strong exogenous factors propel the economy
in the direction of steady expansion. Under this rather one-sided impact, the economy is almost exclusively geared to overheated activity,
full employment, a high level of investment, and remarkably quick
growth. Consequently, the GNP rose by an annual average of 10.6
percent in real terms in the years 1950-70, compared with an average
of 5.5 percent in the countries of the European Economic Community
and 3.3 percent in the United States. Real national income went up
by 10-11 percent per annum, enlarging per capita income from approximately $450 in 1950 to about $1,400 in 1970. Export of goods and
services multiplied by twenty-eight times, amounting to $1,315 million
in 1970 as against $46 million in 1950. And, along with all this, mone-
tary expansion of comparable tempo and scope generated and reinforced
inflationary pressures.

When isolated phenomena of monetary expansion in different
countres are contrasted, there is often the danger of reaching hasty
conclusions by reason, inter alia, of dissimilarities in backgrounds
of development, rates of rising output, propensity to consume and
save, and the population's payment habits. Still, the figures in Table

TABLE 18

Increase in Means of Payment in Selected Countries,
Annual Average for the Years 1950-69
(percentages)

Country	Average Annual Increase	Country	Average Annual Increase
Israel	16.0	Iraq	9.2
Spain	14.0	Australia	9.0
Italy	13.3	Switzerland	8.4
Japan	13.1	Ireland	7.8
Mexico	12.1	Canada	7.5
Portugal	10.6	Belgium	6.8
Iran	10.6	Sweden	6.6
West Germany	10.4	United States	5.6
Denmark	9.2		

18 confirm the fact that, although the differences are many, the rate
at which means of payment in Israel have expanded is among the fastest
in the world.

If we assume that the rate of expansion in means of payment
also reflects in large measure the rate of expansion of total expenditure,
an assumption not far short of reality under the conditions of Israel's
economy, then a wide gap opens between the purchasing power available
and the increment of total resources at fixed prices. Whereupon the
price level rises. The excessive supply of money has been forthcoming
from credit extended to the government by the Central Bank or from
overseas (monetized) as a result of deficit budgetary financing, expansion of credit to the public, and a foreign currency surplus in the overall balance of payments including the capital account, whence followed
monetization of foreign currency and a larger supply of money on the
home market.

Each of these sources has played its part in expanding means of
payment since May 1948, but not uniformly all the time. Up to about
1952, deficits in the state budgets were decisive factors. Between
1953 and 1956, expansion of credit to the public was the chief contribu-
tor. From 1959 onward, accumulation of foreign currency was the
main source of monetary expansion.

It emerges that Israel's condition is in this respect similar to
that of many developing countries which, in search of new capital,
often resort to inflationary methods of financing their economic development. The temptation is hard to resist for governments eager
to bring about compulsory saving by deficit budgeting and thereby
acquire the sinews of investment. The idea that governments can
succeed in so doing is occasionally backed by the argument that, if a
country will not invest in ambitious projects of development, then
ipso facto it resigns itself to economic stagnation, dependence on
outside help to cover the deficits in its balance of payments, and a
low standard of living.

These tendencies were sharpened in Israel by a unique set of
circumstances:

1. A growth of population much larger than in other developing
countries: the period of greatest intensity came immediately after
the establishment of the state, from 1948-52, and this was also
the period of runaway inflation. Even when immigration fell away,
official expenditures on the absorption of immigrants who had entered
in the previous phase were enormous. Many of the newcomers lingered
lengthily on the fringes of the economy in transit camps, without proper
housing or employment. Their economic and social integration by
provision of homes and jobs was the duty of the government. It meant
vast sums for residential and ancillary construction and large new
capital investment to expand productive capacity so that a rapidly
growing population might be assured of livelihood and self-sustaining
economic progress become feasible. The state's development budgets
were the main source of these investments but also the mainspring
of inflationary financing.

2. The geopolitical and military situation made great outlays
on defense obligatory: the defense budget grew from year to year
with the recrudescence of grave and mounting dangers to Israel's
security. Expenditure on armaments also was substantially higher
because of new military and technological developments.

3. In the period 1950-70, bank credit to the public rose by an
annual average of some 20 percent. Inflationary pressures show themselves in the consumer price index, which has risen by an annual

average of 8.9 percent; the pressures were tempered by the swift
growth of the GNP and an immense import surplus which averaged
$459 million annually for the years 1950 through 1970.

However, the average all through fails to reflect fully the differences in general economic and geopolitical conditions from period
to period which accentuated the fluctuations. Thus, the import surplus never exceeded $565 million in the years preceding the Six-Day
War, namely, 1960-66, but in 1970 amounted to $1,261 million by
reason of large defense expenditure with the bulk of it used to pay for
imported military equipment.

Rapid economic growth in conditions of full employment led to
an overheating of the economy—in this ambience of frantic activity,
there was too much liquidity, exaggerated demand, a glut of investment, and overfull employment. The development budget and private
investment injected into the economy funds and projects that outran
the aggregate capacity of all available factors of production.

The measures taken by the government to damp down this over-
expansion were based on control of inflation by restraint of spending
and constraint of effective demand. Far-reaching monetary, fiscal,
and incomes policies were instituted. Price-pegging by every means
short of physical controls was introduced. Competition was encouraged
by liberalization of trade and abolition of administrative restrictions
on imports. Wages and incomes were checked and cartels prohibited.
Open market operations were begun to soak up an overflow of liquidity,
and credit was curtailed.

MONETARY POLICY

The problem here was which of the three main regulators of the
quantity of money in the economy should be preferred in fighting inflation: the rate of interest, open market operations, or reserve requirements.

The political, psychological, and other hindrances to the enforce-
ment of a restrictive monetary policy are formidable. Most of the
time, it is contrary to the interest of the banks because high reserve
requirements diminish their profitability. It clashes with the short-
range wishes of the public, which are on the whole inflationary. Moreover, today a restrictive monetary policy will suffer from the burden
of the tradition of the thirties—the years of stagnation, unemployment,
and deceleration of the pace of economic activity. The conviction to
which those years gave birth, that the cheaper the money and the
lower the interest the better, is now at odds with a policy of restraint,
monetary discipline, and higher interest rates.

Israel's policy thus encounters great difficulties. First of all,
it must always be restrictive and act as a brake; it seldom has a chance
to be a stimulant in times of recession because, under Israel's peculiar
conditions, recessions rarely occur, and thus the image of counter-
cylical action is misshapen and the policy appears to be unbalanced.
An expansionist economic past is hardly a propitious overture to an
efficient monetary policy. Furthermore, the notion prevails that it
is possible to carry out a monetary policy that will be confined to
certain sectors. It is a notion of well-entrenched popularity and it is
difficult to convince public opinion that the economy represents a set
of connected vessels and that, quantitatively and insofar as inflationary
risks are concerned, selectivity does not solve the problems of inflation

The management of interest rates is seriously limited by a high
income tax which provides for deduction of interest in calculating
taxable income and by the slight weight of interest in production costs,
especially in view of the qualitative credit controls which allow a
large volume of credit at concessionary rates for important economic
branches. For interest rates to matter much in Israel, they would
have to be raised to levels that are virtually ruled out for political
and social reasons. And in any case, inflation reduces the real rates
considerably.

Open market operations, using the financial market as a means
of regulating money supply, are of little effect in developing countries
such as Israel: the local market of that potentiality is small and only
took on dimensions of any substance in the years 1962-70.

Consequently, reserve requirements in Israel's banking system
are one of the few effective regulators of the quantity of money. But
evidently this remedy is fiercely resisted by the banks, apprehensive
of their profitability considerations, and also by the public, which
seeks more extensive credit, particularly if inflation prevails. Indeed,
public, political parties, and the press are inclined to support the
expansion of credit, which is thought to be an easy way out of an economic impasse for the public and the individual alike, while its re-
moter and ramified implications are incomprehensible.

In the teeth of this political and civic dissent, a high liquidity
ratio was extensively enforced on the banking system by the Central
Bank. Together with that, as a supplementary instrument of policy,
qualitative credit controls were applied. Lord Boyd-Orr once commented as follows on these controls: "Your monetary policy resem-
bles a system of irrigation—you direct the flow of money just as the
gardener directs the flow of water to the beds that are most in need
of it—to plants that are lagging behind in their growth, and you block
the flow of water where it is excessive."

Qualitative controls were essential as a safety-valve adjunct to the quantitative. When monetary expansion is being throttled, there is a danger that at a certain point shortage of credit may give rise to a public reaction that in the last resort might entail a cancellation of all credit restrictions, with all its attendant risks. That hazard is counteracted by extending credit on concessionary terms to essential branches of the economy, and first and foremost for financing the expansion of exports.

As to the institutional form of qualitative controls, the widespread view that a state central bank would be less efficient and less flexible in credit allocation than commercial banks is not upheld by experience in Israel. Generally speaking, the Central Bank (the Bank of Israel) has a wider conspectus of the interests of the state and a broader spectrum of macro-economic information and can establish a proper scale of priorities. If it is entrusted with the task of qualitative controls, the division of labor is clear: it takes care of the macro-economic elements, the commercial banks deal with the micro-economic considerations as affecting applicants—profitability, satisfactory management, creditworthiness, type of collateral, and the like.

These principles and this concern for the balance of payments, determining as they do the scale of priorities for allocation of credit, guide the policy of qualitative control and are in great part instrumental in assuring an adequate supply of money to those branches that matter most for economic growth; quantitative controls reduce the speed of inflationary monetary expansion.

FISCAL POLICY

Fiscal policy could not and did not contribute notably to control of inflation. The government had recourse to inflationary financing because of the requirements of defense, particularly since 1967, the absorption and economic integration of immigrants, political and social pressures that swelled the welfare budget and social expenditure, large allocations for subsidies to prevent too steep a rise in the cost-of-living index (this is an integral part of the incomes policy), and resultant wage claims.

A distinct and permanent feature of fiscal policy was the development budget, its size reflecting a faith that furtherance and acceleration of economic growth are indispensable to absorption of immigrants and the pursuit of social welfare schemes that only an expanding economy could sustain. Expenditure on development is not fully disclosed in the state budget since a number of development institutions established by the government, such as the Agricultural, the Industrial Development

Banks and mortgage banks financing housing, raise capital on their own account on the domestic and external markets; these far from inconsiderable sums are not included in the state budget.

The budgetary deficits,* which were nil between the years 1964/65 and 1966/67, were swollen by the war expenditure of 1967 to an average of $326 million for each of the years 1967/68 to 1969/70.

Budgetary expenditure fell into four main categories: the defense budget, the development budget, the social and administrative budget, and debt repayment. Table 19 shows the composition of the government budget for 1970/71 in absolute amounts and percentages.

The development budgets were mainly financed by funds raised abroad which came to $3 billion in 1971, partly in gifts, partly as added foreign indebtedness. Inflationary pressure, with all its implications for price levels and balance of payments, was persistent and pronounced.

TABLE 19

Composition of the Government Budget for 1970/71,
by Main Categories

Category	$ million	Percentage
Defense budget	1,472	46.3
Development budget[a]	405	12.7
Social and administrative budget	1,032	32.5
Debt repayment	268	8.5
Total	3,177	100.0

Note: Figures include additional budgets.

[a]Including residential housing and public construction; excluding debt repayment.

----

*Defined here as the difference between income from taxes, dues, interest, government enterprises and property in the ordinary and development budgets, and expenditure in the ordinary budget.

Table 20 shows the contribution of foreign currency accruals to state budget, by added indebtedness for three years typical of the pre-war and postwar periods—1963/64, 1966/67, and 1970/71. This expansionism of fiscal policy, as already emphasized, could scarcely be avoided under geopolitical and social pressures, and given the need for an incomes policy that depended largely on subsidies to keep prices stable and minimize payment of cost-of-living allowances.

Revenues dropped behind the ever greater exigencies of external and internal policy. Direct taxation rose to very high levels particularly on marginal incomes, sometimes as much as 71.9 percent of income. Moreover, the high rates started at quite modest incomes: for a family of four with an annual income of $3,600, the marginal tax is almost 40 percent; for a similar family with an income of $6,500, almost 60 percent; and for one with an income of $11,000, nearly 72 percent. In the course of time, these taxes became counterproductive and were a disincentive of extra labor effort and the growth of the GNP.

The customs tariff policy has been very selective, at times in a slant toward the overprotection of infant industry, so that inefficient enterprises were sheltered and spared competition. This policy was modified in the late 1960's in favor of liberalization and a gradual contraction of protective tariffs.

Revenue duties also are high and very selective, imposing a heavy burden on what may be considered luxury goods, sometimes in lieu of adjusting exchange rates to reality. On the other hand, a very substantial proportion of imports has been exempted from customs duty or subjected only to nominal charges. This pronounced differentiation of tariffs somewhat distorted the pattern of the newly established

TABLE 20

Contributions of Foreign Currency Accruals to
State Budget, 1963-64, 1966-67, and 1970-71

Year	$ million*
1963-64 (performance)	157
1966-67 (performance)	190
1970-71 (proposal)	510

*Including counterpart funds in connection with U.S. food surpluses.

body economic and hardly aided any attempt to use fiscal policy extensively as an instrument against inflation and for countercyclical purposes.

CONCLUSIONS

In Israel, recessionary tendencies in the business cycle are
weakened by a large capital import and a rapid demographic expansion
by immigration. Thus, very little room is left for a countercyclical
policy which by its nature operates in two directions: restricting and
restraining in periods of buoyant activity, stimulating and accelerating
in slumps. It is therefore extremely difficult for the Treasury and
the Central Bank to adopt the policy of moderating monetary expansion.
Politically, it is extremely difficult to apply the brakes all the time
and never press the accelerator. After all, if economic activity ap-
peared to be sagging, large capital inflow and immigration revived it,
but a continuous policy of restraint distorts the image of the monetary
authorities in the public eye.

Nevertheless, the need to pursue drastic monetary and fiscal
policies became progressively acuter as the program of import liberalization went forward and the physical and administrative controls
of the first three years of the state were dismantled. The ideological
tendency toward unlimited expansion prevalent in Israel's society and
economy militates against a policy of restraint concerned with the
internal equilibrium and balanced economic growth. Still, two facts
favor the application of such a policy: (1) the most drastic of measures
does not produce a deflationary crisis for the economy is always stimulated by large capital import and the pace of growth, accordingly, is
sustained, and (2) it is possible to shift without much delay from re-
trenchment to expansion since the changeover arouses neither political
nor social resistance.

Many psychological and social, political and institutional circumstances and attitudes militate against a consistently restrictive monetary, fiscal, and incomes policy. The forbidding objective constraints
of heavy defense spending and mass immigration are even more formidable. Despite these odds, the government determinedly embarked
upon such a policy, and not without success. Indeed, as noted, the
economy is by and large marked by full employment, a substantial
development budget, and a mounting volume of investment with more
investment plans and money pouring in, even though no idle factors
of production are presently available.

Of this situation there can be three possible consequences:

1. Open inflation, monetary expansion, extra purchasing power and real expenditure, and also higher prices for goods and services which might absorb part of the excess liquidity and so help toward an equilibrium, but then costs of production would go up and affect Israel's exports and its competitive economic capacity, and the upshot would be an even more adverse balance of payments and exhaustion of foreign currency reserves.

2. Suppressed inflation—an artificial maintenance of price stability by administrative controls while expansion persists and the growth of purchasing power and real expenditure continues. Consumption would rise rapidly because of the disparity between excess purchasing power and the available supply of deliberately cheapened goods and services. Moreover, excess purchasing power would mean more imports and an extensive and expanding black market, ultimately inflicting irreparable damage on the entire economy. Suppressed inflation always boomerangs, and its detrimental effect would ultimately be bound to force the abandonment of such a policy.

3. A policy of saturation—total liberalization of imports with a lowering of tariffs and maintenance of price stability at the cost of a big jump in imports. Foreign currency reserves would ebb to the vanishing point, and in the long run production would suffer because of the impossibility of financing its high import component (fuel, spare parts, raw materials).

If action climaxing in open or suppressed inflation or saturation is thus ruled out, the only workable policy was to combat inflation of costs and demand alike, and the deterrents used were monetary and fiscal measures and a check on the rise of incomes. Prices were kept down by every possible device except physical controls, namely, by stepping up competition, liberalizing trade, abolishing administrative restrictions, pegging wages, raising taxes, issuing compulsory loans, tightening credit, and operating on the open market.

These barriers against what might have proved a very serious situation were fortified by the currency devaluations of 1949, 1952, 1953, 1962, 1967, and 1971. Each readjustment helped to reinstate a modicum of equilibrium, although only until incomes, wages, and prices caught up with the new rates and started the inflationary process all over again. But matters would have been much graver without these devaluations, and adverse repercussions on economic growth inescapable. The experience demonstrated the rationale of a certain flexibility of exchange rates, especially under conditions of very rapid economic growth.

Control of inflation in Israel was perhaps less than adequate, but it did slow down the inflationary spiral and spared the country's economic growth the more damaging effects of that spiral. Heavy taxation could not eliminate budgetary deficits in a perplexing period of mass immigration and geopolitical predicaments that necessarily led to large defense expenditures; however, it did contract their dimensions. Moreover, apart from taxation, the encouragement of savings by the issue of government securities linked to foreign currency and the cost-of-living index, quantitative and qualitative credit controls, and, by no means least, the series of currency devaluations each made its contribution to whatever containment of inflationary pressures was achieved.

NOTE

1. The OECD Observer, 1971.

8

The economic and social structure of Israel, then, is distinguished by a multiplicity of different and variegated socioeconomic
systems in coexistence. The government, private, and cooperative
sectors live together in an economy that is geared to the general aims
and broad objectives of the state. Huge amounts of public and investment capital are the basis for the growth of so kaleidoscopic an economy
with its unique division into three sectors. Outside the Soviet bloc,
the division is public and private only. In Israel, the workers' sector,
partly cooperative and partly directed or controlled by the Labour
Federation (Histadrut), is large enough to be an autonomous element.

Haim Barkai uses the following definition:

We classify the various economic units into three, instead
of the "conventional" two—the public and private sectors,
because the latter classification, though useful in study-
ing the economy of many other countries, is not fully suit-
able to conditions in Israel. Israel's peculiarity in this
respect is a result of the role of the Histadrut, the General Federation of Labour.

The Histadrut functions of course as a trade union—
it is, for all purposes, the trade union of Israel. . . .
But in addition to its traditional role as an organization
of workers, it has a direct stake in production. It is the
owner of production units in various branches of the economy, and also serves as a parent body for other production units, organized as cooperatives—moshavim, and
collectives—kibbutzim.

The identification of the production units connected
with the Histadrut as a distinct group is primarily on a

113

social and political basis. But it is also significant in
terms of economic behavior since, in theory at any rate,
the activities of the Histadrut production units are not
exclusively motivated by consideration of profit. In this
respect they resemble publicly-owned rather than privately-owned production units.[1]

A labor sector in which workers are employers and employees
as well emerged from ideological motivations and economic conditions.
The immigrants of the first two decades of the twentieth century were
steeped in the doctrines of the pre-World War I revolutionary movement in Russia yet had despaired of the possibility that Jews could
become part and parcel of the Gentile society of Europe. Some were
immersed in the idealistic current of that movement and were pro-
foundly influenced by Tolstoyan ideas and spiritual values. Others
were disillusioned to see the movement planning to reconstruct society
from above by state control of means of production, with no fundamental change in the individual style and quality of life; they aspired to
build a new society—a labor community founded in new moral and
national concepts. The thinking of a Jewish Socialist, Ber Borochov,
based on a synthesis of Zionism and Socialism to be realized in Palestine, cast a strong spell upon them. Borochov saw an occupational
redirection, a return to labor and manual labor at that, within an
autonomous community in Palestine, as the only way to national and
social normalization of Jewish life.

There were also economic and national considerations at work.
Wherever modern industrialism began to evolve many years ago, a
workers' class, as an organic part of society, was gradually formed
in the course of generations. In this lengthy process, class and occupational delimitations have been continuous and rigid. In many
developing countries, more recently and rapidly, industrialized and
urbanized, the workers' class has been built up within a single generation by a shift from village to town. The workers' class in Israel
is of different nature and origin. It is the product not of an urbanization of the rural economy but mainly of immigration and an occupational
reshuffle.

Most Diaspora Jews were engaged in trade or the liberal professions. A minor part was declassed, without any strictly defined
calling. The transformation of immigrants from this milieu into a
class of workers has been, economically, technically, and psychologi-
cally, among the basic designs in the social and economic pattern of
Israel, although understandably the training of men and women bereft
of any tradition of manual labor to perform skilled jobs in the new
factories and farmsteads could not help but entail a certain waste and
an uneconomic expenditure of money and effort. There was also the

complication of new forms of living, such as the collective commune, which were impracticable except on an agricultural basis.

Thus, economic, social, and psychological factors merged and interacted in a shift of the whole economic and occupational direction of the immigrants, and the workers' class sprang chiefly not from the farming community but from the towns: its progenitor is not the landless peasant but the lower-middle class.

Inexperienced, in a region largely desert, swamp, and barren slopes, competing with backward but cheap Arab labor, in an economy still embryonic, the newcomers were under objective compulsion not only to seek employment in a narrow and underdeveloped labor market but also, and at the same time, to find autonomous employment for themselves. This necessity to create their own labor market, conjoined with the ideological tenets that the young society embraced, led to the founding of collective farming communities (kibbutzim), cooperatives, and economic undertakings by the Labour Federation in agriculture, industry, finance, and transport, all shaping new socioeconomic forms. Public funds, fed largely by collection from Diaspora Jewry, helped the Labour Federation in its task.

The immigration of labor preceded economic growth and it was among the newcomers that the idea germinated of producing their own demand for labor, of being their own employers, of establishing an independent labor economy. The idea had already taken practical form in the pre-state era, but it became much more intense afterward. Thus it happened that certain key positions in the economy that either held no attraction for private capital (such as mixed farming) or were occupied by labor from the outset (such as transport) came to be an integral part of this new economy of workers. Some of these positions, such as the virtually monopolistic control of building exercised by labor in the early days, had to be surrendered as private capital gradually penetrated them. But in essence, despite a certain loss of influence, the labor economy has been carried over into the new environment, sometimes in competition and sometimes in cooperation with private enterprise.

By reason of this two-tiered sociological edifice, Israel's workingclass is not entirely made up of hired wage-earners. A sizable proportion engaged in mixed farming are neither peasants, in the usual sense of the word, not ordinary hired hands. They live and work in collective or cooperative farms or in joint enterprises run with varying degrees of cooperation. The farms range in type from smallholders' villages, with joint sale and purchase, joint use of machinery, national ownership of the land, and a ban on hired labor, to the all-out collective commune, with joint production and consumption on the principle

"From each according to his capacity, to each according to his needs," as far as the means and possibilities of the village will allow. In these collectives, cooperation is total and marks every walk of life—communal kitchens, dining halls, and children's houses are the rule, and no direct wages are paid.

The members of the transport and producers' cooperatives in city and town are the urban counterparts of the independent agricultural workers. The cooperatives are no different constitutionally from the usual producers' cooperatives of the West, but numerically and economically they are much more important in Israel.

There are also several economic institutions established directly by the Labour Federation: these are neither cooperative nor collective groups but economic concerns financed by the capital of the trade unions themselves.

The ordinary wage-earner and the independent worker operate side by side in every area, and there is inevitably a perpetual interchange from one group to the other. In the same farm village, for example, a wage-earning group of laborers who work in privately-owned orange groves may coexist with a collective self-employed group tending its groves. Similarly, in the towns a workers' cooperative bakery may operate in competition with a private bakery that employs hired labor. A further complication is the intermediate sort of worker who combines a private job with membership in a cooperative: he hands over the wage that he earns to his group, which is organized along collective lines and is often engaged in some production of its own as well.

Over the years, collective and labor enterprise has fallen off, relatively speaking, but in absolute terms its expansion has been uninterrupted, and this for two reasons—economic and ideological. In the struggle against natural and economic adversity, the pooling of strength and resources provides a powerful weapon, which explains why collective groups may also be encountered in other lands of new settlement where, as in Israel, natural conditions are difficult. In Israel, that handicap was magnified by the transition from one class, and in most cases from one occupation, to another. Mutual aid, training and other such means are facilitated in large measure by collectivity. The ideological motivation is the wish of the workers to create the nucleus of a new society, a wish to some extent fulfilled thanks to the special conditions that a pioneer movement brings into being.

The dimensions in quantity of the three sectors of Israel's economy have been investigated by Haim Barkai. If the GDP is tabulated by sectoral employment, the result is not very different from that yielded by tabulation by net product yields, that is, there are no apparent discrepancies of sectoral productivity to justify an assessment of efficiency correlations. This correspondence between the three sectors in respect of the number of employed and their net product is shown in Table 21.

Contact among the three sectors is sometimes expressed in cooperation on a basis of mutual interest and sometimes in conflict, but most of the time in a rewarding coexistence. In almost all areas, the powerful elements of intersectoral competition are visible.

The order of magnitude of the public sector is determined by a large import of capital channeled through the government and the national institutions, by the need to lay down the infrastructure of an undeveloped country speedily yet securely, and also, and far from

TABLE 21

Net Domestic Product and Employment, by Sector, Selected Years, 1953-60

	Total Economy	Public Sector	Histadrut Sector	Private Sector
1. Net Domestic Product	(percentage)			
1953	100.0	19.4	20.3	60.3
1957	100.0	20.9	20.6	58.5
1958	100.0	20.0	20.0	60.0
1959	100.0	21.6	20.3	58.1
1960	100.0	21.1	20.4	58.5
2. Employment, 1959				
Thousands	675.4	119.2	152.6	403.6
Percentage	100.0	17.6	22.6	59.8

Source: Haim Barkai, The Public, Histadrut and Private Sectors in the Israel Economy (Jerusalem: Falk Institute, 1968), Tables 1 and 5.

least, by the circumstance that the economy of Israel is being propelled by a conscious effort to realize a national political set of objectives, and not by the forces of normal economic gravitation alone.
Consequently, the profit motive in the public sector is relegated to
second place and the scale of priorities is influenced primarily by
the task that the sector is committed to perform in the attainment of
national-political ends. Not inconsiderable economic losses are
involved at the outset of settlement and development thus conceived,
and particularly in the branches of the economy that are not profitable
in the initial period yet are essential for economic growth.

The private sector was swayed a good deal by the entry of entrepreneurs who wanted, indeed needed, to develop their undertakings
in a land of their absorption, but always with due heed to economic
considerations of profitability, stability and expectations.

Any final verdict as to the success of this socioeconomic polymorphic experiment in Israel is still premature. It seems that the
philosophy behind this maelstrom of cross-currents is ideological
and pragmatic in one, a reflection of conditions of economy and society.
Its rationale is a national awareness that, if there is to be organic
growth of a polymorphic society, the three sectors must coexist.

This polymorphia, the like of which is not to be found elsewhere,
has enriched the quality of life in Israel. It adds a new dimension to
existence: the freedom of every man or woman to independently choose
the way of life and the vocation that harmonize best with individual
aspirations and aptitudes. The coexistence of different socioeconomic
forms—now in conjunction, now in collision, but always in competition—
is a weighty spiritual and economic factor, in the growth of Israel's
economy.

NOTE

1. Haim Barkai, The Public, Histadrut and Private Sectors in
the Israel Economy (Jerusalem: Maurice Falk Institute for Economic
Research in Israel, December 1968).

Difficulties and disparities in the balance of payments are among the vexing impediments of economic growth in developing countries. Shortage of foreign currency may hinder the growth by contracting imports, particularly imports of capital goods, essential raw materials, and other inputs of current production. The problem can take on more ominous proportions in a country like Israel, with a high import component of production on account of the scarcity of natural resources and with a rapidly growing population whose integration in the economic processes of production and expansion is bound to lag behind demography so that in the interim period current consumption must depend largely on imports. The repercussions of this contraction of essential imports on employment and output would therefore compound the impact of those factors on economic growth.

One the other hand, a second industrial revolution is taking place in the world, fraught with consequences no less far-reaching than the first two centuries ago. Its salient phenomenon is less importance of natural resources and greater relative weight of the human element—skill and know-how, education and technology.

Per Jacobson, Managing Director of the International Monetary Fund, stated:

> In the highly industrialized countries, expansion of output has been heavily concentrated on more complicated manufactured goods, such as machinery, electrical goods, aircraft, etc., with a relatively low raw material content, which has limited the demand for raw materials. . . . One important change of great significance for the industrial regions is the gradual decline in recent years

in the average amount of raw materials and fuel required
per unit of manufacturing production.

This development points to a rising demand for capital. The new
sophisticated industries are capital-intensive; thus, each worker
controls a much larger amount of capital equipment and manual labor
is decreasing. It follows that voluminous imports of capital goods
at the start of development and growth bear significantly on the balance
of payments.

The economic history of Israel is mirrored more visibly in the
development of its foreign trade than in any other single facet of the
economy, and the apparent abnormalities there, unavoidable concomitants of special conditions and an unusual rate of progress, are
as follows: exceptional size of trade per capita, a large adverse
trade balance, and—but Israel shares this characteristic with many
developing countries—the high proportion of capital goods imported,
accounting for 21.3 percent of total imports in the years 1950-70.
These features are really aspects of one and the same circumstance:
Israel is a young and swiftly advancing country, and large imports
and an adverse trade balance are concomitants of progress. With a
strong inflow of immigrants and rapid economic growth, home production cannot keep pace with what a growing population needs in consumption goods and the apparatus of production. Until the new branches
of production are set in motion, the newcomers who are put to work to
expand productive capacity must be fed, clothed, and housed by imported goods, which means that a substantial part of imports is in
essence capital investment, but a part of the consumption goods imported to satisfy the needs of those same newcomers who are employed
in the investment sector of the economy is also investment.

Thus, foreign trade is a very sensitive and important index in
a period of development since the capital equipment, at least in the
first stage, must be imported to expand production. Therefore, any
rise in investment will be reflected in import statistics, which will
also reflect any rise or change in consumption, particularly if a
certain time lag between increment of population and increment of
production is taken into account. Further, as propounded, the larger
production probably will not be confined to supplying the home market
in a small country with scarce natural resources that can hardly be
self-sufficient and must find the requital for foodstuffs, raw materials,
and capital goods not locally produced. A series of indexes of import,
export, and import of capital goods is shown in Table 22. The data
for the years 1967-70 reflect the distorting effects of the war of 1967
and its requirements.

Israel's economic development policy is influenced by the as-
piration, indeed urgent necessity, to reach an equilibrium in the

TABLE 22

Indexes of Import, Export, and Import of Capital Goods, 1950-70

Year	Current Account		Total Import of Capital Goods ($million)
	Import	Export	
1950	328	46	n.a
1951	426	67	n.a
1952	393	86	87
1953	365	102	68
1954	373	135	57
1955	427	144	64
1956	535	178	91
1957	557	222	117
1958	569	235	76
1959	602	286	114
1960	696	359	105
1961	857	425	151
1962	958	503	143
1963	1,011	607	142
1964	1,225	658	197
1965	1,238	711	179
1966	1,272	832	193
1967	1,440	908	130
1968	1,865	1,146	231
1969	2,150	1,256	282
1970	2,580	1,315	348

balance of payments within the foreseeable future. No other policy will answer the doubts as to whether the present volume of capital imports can be sustained or stand up to heavy defense expenditure with its high foreign currency component and, at the same time, express the national will to match political with economic independence.

Liberalization of foreign trade, exposing Israel's manufacture to the competition of imports and the efforts to penetrate world markets, are signs of the economy's endeavor to balance its foreign currency income and expenditure and adapt its pattern of development to universal trends with a view to the advantages of economies of scale. In practice, for Israel this means producing import substitutes and expanding exports quickly. Meanwhile, the gap between the overall balance of payments, including capital account and current

balance of payments, has been very wide and precedents for it elsewhere would be hard to discover.

If the years of war and near-war (1967-70) are excluded since
their economic content was affected by imports of war materials and
arms, the overall balance of payments—with the exception of a trien-
nium of negligible deficit—was in the black all through the period 1950-
66, and reserves of foreign currency amounting to some $600 million
at the end of 1966 could be accumulated. By contrast, the current
balance of payments was in the red all along and the excess of imports
over visible and invisible exports, namely, the cumulative value of
unrequited imports, came to $6.4 billion: the excess of imports over
exports was $532 million in 1967, $718 million in 1968, $894 million
in 1969, and $1,265 million in 1970. Israel's peculiar geopolitical
conditions had much to do with inflating its import bill even in peace
time, as a function of military preparedness.

Immense capital import, $10 billion in the twenty years reviewed,
is the key to an understanding of the conditions of Israel's economy.
At the same time, it has been a positive factor, although not the only
factor of significance in Israel's economic growth. The dependence
of that growth on imports was thus absolute, at least initially.

But this extraordinary supply of external capital is by no means
indefinitely assured. Therefore, progress toward emancipation from
total reliance on unrequited imports and toward economic independence
is essential. After the first hectic development made possible by
massive infusion of capital some readjustment of the balance of payments is a matter of urgency, involving more capital formation by
savings and accumulation and a higher level of self-sufficiency in
satisfying the current needs of the population, as well as much larger
exports.

The time gap between investment and its maturing adds to the
difficulty of readjustment since in that interval the sources of external assistance and credit that nurture economic growth might con-
ceivably dwindle into insignificance. Yet until the Six-Day War, the
progress of readjustment was remarkable. It can be quantified and
measured by two decisive criteria: the ratio of exports to imports
and the share of the import surplus in Israel's total resources.

Until 1966, the ratio of exports to imports exhibited a steady
climb toward a balance in the current account. In 1952, export
receipts covered only 22 percent of the value of imports, the rest
being financed by capital imports; in 1960, the figure was 50 percent
and in 1966 it had risen to 66 percent. True, 1966 was a year of
recession with concurrent curtailment of imports, and it hardly

represents the whole period, but despite that qualification the progress is unmistakable. And even if a small amount of unrequited imports persisted as a residual element in the balance of payments, there would scarcely be any real difficulty in financing a deficit of that size. The war of 1967 naturally slowed down this progress because of military imports, and in 1970 the ratio of exports to imports dropped to 52 percent.

Even a more conclusive proof of readjustment is the changing share of the import surplus in Israel's total resources, comprising the GNP and the excess of imports over exports on current account. The pattern that emerges appears similar to that resulting from the export-import ratio. In 1950, excess of imports over exports was 40 percent of total resources; in 1956, 23 percent; in 1960, some 15 percent; and in 1966—once more qualified in the light of recession in that year—10 percent. All this was accomplished together with a spectacular rise in the standard of living.

Reversal in 1970 was sharp: the share of the import surplus in total resources went up to 20 percent. Still, a return to where foreign trade and balance of payments stood before the Six-Day War could, within a few years, start the process of readjustment moving surely again.

Here a new problem arises: integration in world markets. To improve the balance of payments it is necessary, in the main, to expand exports. Exports did indeed rise from $46 million in 1950 to $1,315 million in 1970, but imports also went up. It is a question of the ability to compete in world markets and, as long as physical expansion was proceeding apace, this question was rather neglected apart from the fact that inflation is not without its detrimental effect on that ability.

Between 1953 and 1959, imports rose each year by an average of 6 percent; between 1960 and 1965 by 13 percent; in each of the years 1966 and 1967 by 8.4 percent; and annually from 1968 to 1970 by 22 percent. Exports rose each year by an average of 18.7 percent from 1953 to 1959; by 16 percent from 1960 to 1965; by 13 percent in 1966 and 1967; and by 14 percent between 1968 and 1970.

The distinction between the exports of Israel and those of other developing countries is obvious: nearly 90 percent of income from exports in other developing countries is yielded by shipments of raw materials, including food, whereas the corresponding figure in the exports of Israel is 24 percent while industrial products account for 76 percent of income from exports. The distribution of Israel's exports of goods in 1961 and 1970 shows the same tendency toward

TABLE 23

Exports of Goods,
by Main Groups, 1961 and 1970

	1961		1970	
	$ million	percentage	$ million	percentage
Citrus	40.5	17.0	83.0	11.6
Other farm products	22.5	9.5	43.4	6.1
Diamonds	64.9	27.3	202.9	28.4
Textiles	24.4	10.3	96.3	13.5
Mining	13.4	5.6	43.4	6.1
Citrus products	7.9	3.3	35.1	4.9
Other industries	64.2	27.0	210.0	29.4
Total	237.8	100.0	714.1	100.0

TABLE 24

Exports of Services,
by Main Groups, 1961 and 1970

	1961		1970	
	$ million	percentage	$ million	percentage
Tourism	30.1	16.8	103.5	15.9
Transport	84.5	47.3	261.6	40.2
Insurance	25.3	14.2	116.3	17.9
Capital services	13.1	7.3	52.7	8.1
Government	7.5	4.2	28.0	4.3
Others	18.1	10.2	88.3	13.6
Total	178.6	100.0	650.4	100.0

diversification (see Table 23), while exports of services expanded even more (see Table 24).

Evidently then, Israel's economic growth was sped decisively by import of capital which opened a gap between current and overall balances of payments and strengthened the prospects for balancing the current account. The import surplus indispensably conditioned that growth by virtue of the lapse of time between the arrival of new-comers and their integration in the country's labor force and economy, and between investment and its maturing. Until the Six-Day War, economic growth and maturity of investment made for a steady approach to an equilibrium in the balance of payments whether the criterion is the export-import ratio or the share of the import surplus in total resources.

EFFECTS OF POLITICAL AND MILITARY
EVENTS ON ISRAEL'S ECONOMY

The rhythm and directions of Israel's economy in the period 1967-70 were determined and dominated by political and military events. Idle factors and underutilized capacity of production were galvanized once more by an effective demand. This demand, generated by the war effort, absorbed as much as a quarter of the GNP, and an artificial extra-economic sector came into being to take up the rapidly rising output.

In those years, the economy was chiefly characterized by a susceptibility to strong pressures upon limited resources, capacity of production, and manpower. The volume of investments was immense, but without it the state could not have carried the burden of security expenditure in the future. Expansion of investment was essential to ensure that the vastly greater defense spending should not add to the weight of that spending within total outlays, for any increase would have left little for other uses. Current absorption of immigration, although it was not as multitudinous as in the first years of the state, required an enormously higher expenditure per family and person owing to its changed pattern: cultural and economic backgrounds and standards of living were very different in the affluent countries of origin and in Israel.

These pressures made themselves felt in overemployment. A real shortage of labor sent up wages and salaries, with detrimental impacts upon the price levels and competitiveness of the economy, and deterioration of labor relations. Purchasing power, and with it consumption, expanded. The remedy of confining consumption and diverting production to the war effort and exports was not applied vigorously enough or with sufficient effect. Political and psychological factors were involved, for in a democratic state a certain degree of consensus is indispensable to carry out a policy that is at variance with short-term interests and expectations. In the long run, restraint and regulation can avert much suffering but there is no doubt that in the short run they are uncomfortable and inconvenient. Moreover, misconception and misunderstanding of the economic processes, and errors in grasping their complex and intricate implications, are equally a handicap to the shaping of any rational and sensible economic plan.

From June 1967 until 1971, despite the urgency of channeling overall production to continuing security needs and tasks, per capita consumption rose by some 20 percent, which was much too much. Indeed, the rate of climb in 1968-69, some 11 percent in total consumption and 8 percent per capita, was one of the highest; between 1960 and 1968, private consumption had risen on the average by only 5 percent per annum. How the economically unwelcome extra purchasing power, drawn from overfull employment and, in its sequel, from higher incomes, led to greater consumption is shown in Table 25. As to money supply, after a rapid rise in 1966 and 1967, due to reflationary policy and the Six-Day War, its growth slowed down in 1968 and 1969 but increased again in 1970, as shown in Table 26. The deceleration in 1968 and 1969 can be attributed to depletion of foreign currency reserves by $330 million in the two years, reducing the liquidity of banks and thus restricting the growth of money supply; in 1970, this did not happen.

In this critical context, the detrimental effect was a further maladjustment in an already strained balance of payments. Corrective internal policies are the only remedy in such a case: to restore a measure of equilibrium in the overall balance of payments is far from impossible, but it requires a countercyclical policy to restrain and decelerate economic activity in booms and quicken it in recessions.

A significant cut of defense expenditures was practically excluded. A simple demographic comparison of opposing forces shows that 3 million Israelis are in direct military contact with 60 million Arabs in neighboring states. Much of this numerical disparity can be offset only by higher-grade technology, in other words, by the technical skill to use various means of waging war and military equipment of great power and effectiveness, all of which are of course very costly.

No wonder then that, in the state budget of IL 11, 119 million in 1970/71, Il 5, 152 million, or 46. 3 percent, was allocated to defense. Plainly, that sum could not be found out of current revenues, on top of high investment and the great expense of absorbing and integrating

TABLE 25

Growth of Real Total and Per Capita
Consumption, 1967-70
(percentages)

	Total	Per Capita
1967	1.4	-1.7
1968	12.0	8.3
1969	11.7	9.0
1970	5.1	2.3

TABLE 26

Money Supply, 1967-70

	Balance at End of Year (IL million)	Percentage Increase in End-Year Balance	Average Annual Balance (IL million)
1967	2,538.5	26.4	2,366.4
1968	2,898.5	14.2	2,814.9
1969	2,970.1	2.5	3,015.4
1970	2,389.8	14.1	3,167.3

new immigrants. Thus, the needs of economic development and part
of the cost of social services had to be met by funds from abroad,
contributed mainly by Jewish communities, and by an increase of the
national debt.

In this conjuncture, the three years following the Six-Day War
were distinguished by unremitting and on the whole successful efforts
to neutralize pressures by increasing national output and expanding
the economy. The GNP rose by 35 percent in real terms between
the middle of 1967 and the end of 1970, the volume of investment in

that period was IL 13, 800 million at 1970 prices, and 100, 000 immigrants arrived, somewhat easing the shortage of manpower. In 1967,
there were still untapped reserves of production factors, and from
June of that year onward an increment of some 30, 000 workers was
being regularly provided by the administered areas. Moreover, the
huge scale of capital imports and the decline in foreign currency
reserves were instrumental as powerful accelerants of economic
growth, and more and more factors of production were activated as
capital equipment began to be imported in quantity.

To these stimuli and activation of productive capacity, Israel
owed its sustained height of economic performance and its speed of
economic expansion, coinciding with a military campaign of major
intensity. It was the response to a challenge without precedent in
the history of Israel or, for that matter, of any other country.

These developments reflected once again the decisive role that
effective demand bears on economic growth. Demand, rising with
spectacular rapidity and always a few steps ahead of expansion of
output, galvanized all branches of the economy. Industry worked to
full capacity for the war effort and for a civilian market that had to
cater to the much larger private consumption that full employment
and bigger incomes allowed. The building trade was booming in
answer to the requirements of a more numerous immigration accustomed to higher standards of housing. Rising exports took part of
a production that became more competitive thanks to economies of
scale, inflation in export markets, and a spillover of technological
know-how from Israel's military establishment. Food production
expanded to meet the larger domestic demand. The off-season
demand in Western Europe for Israel-grown vegetables, fruit, and
flowers was rewarding: it reflected higher continental incomes and
consequent luxury buying, as well as the effectiveness of Israel's
new methods of cultivation and marketing.

Therefore, the new conditions might be defined as a replica
of the earlier boom and economic growth of which the transplantation
process was the principal driving force. That process is now of
less weight within what has become a fairly broad economy; in part,
it has been replaced by the stimulus of the war effort and a proliferation of investment, and expanding public and private consumption.
Yet basically this analysis is virually identical with that of the period
of transplantation, but it fails to explain how such an expanding demand, created by a convergence of extra-economic currents (war,
immigration, and large-scale investment) could be effectively satisfied. The determining factor was a substantial rise in the import
surplus which was paid for by import of capital, by growth of the
external debt, and by contraction of foreign currency reserves.

In 1969, when foreign currency reserves declined precipitously, a red light of warning flashed before Israel's economy. These reserves safeguard the economic and military operations of the state. It is true that until 1968 there was a considerable deficit on current balance, but the overall balance of payments showed a surplus. In 1968 and 1969, however, there was also, for the first time, a large deficit in the overall balance. Foreign currency reserves increased for as long as that balance showed a surplus, as long as capital imports of all types exceeded the deficit on current balance, but in 1968-69 they declined by $330 million as imports were not sufficient to finance the excess of imports over exports.

Stabilization and even some increase of reserves were achieved as soon as import of capital rose again, not only with larger receipts from abroad in gifts and sales of Independence Loan but also with a general rise in state indebtedness, which in 1971 amounted to $3,000 million—a very high level considering not only the population but also the national output, whose future yield is thereby heavily mortgaged.

In these several ways, by rapid economic growth and a rising import surplus alike, the resources were found to meet the larger effective demand for goods and services. On the other hand, pressure on limited resources has led to an appreciable slowing down in the annual pace of export progress—from 27.3 percent in 1968 to 7.5 percent in 1969 and 9.1 percent in 1970. However, the trend reversed in 1971: in the first half of that year, exports rose by 21 percent as against only 4.6 percent in the corresponding half of 1970. But the developments in 1967-70 had widened the gap in the balance of payments mainly by substantial imports for defense purposes, which added largely to the import surplus so that the policy target of economic independence receded despite the increase in exports.

Therefore, distribution of incremental resources assumes a major significance. In 1970, the increment came to IL 2,605 million, of which private consumption absorbed 13 percent, public consumption (mainly for defense needs) 54 percent, gross investment 14 percent, and exports 19 percent. This was much better than 1969, when private consumption absorbed 39 percent, public consumption 27 percent, gross investment 21 percent, and exports 13 percent. The change reflects the diversion of production from private consumption to the requirements of the defense effort with investment maintaining its high level.

The varying percentages of course have a bearing on the economic policies and the fiscal and monetary measures of the government and the Central Bank, directed as they are to intensifying the shift from private consumption to public consumption, exports, and

investment. These moves did not uniformly succeed because of the
precarious geopolitical situation in the Middle East.

As the deficit in the balance of payments went on growing, steps
of economic policy were taken to check demand in the civilian sector:
the government and the Central Bank are applying economic restraints
to repress the growth of the import surplus on the current account
and to prevent a further depletion of foreign currency reserves.

THE ADMINISTERED AREAS

The assumption that effective demand is the chief and most
significant incentive and agent of economic growth finds confirmation
in developments in the areas administered by Israel since the Six-
Day War.

The unique and unprecedented policy of "open bridges" encourages trade between these areas and Arab states that are still at war
with Israel, and expands and variegates the agricultural production
in the administered areas. Agricultural production there is steadily
and systematically fostered and extended by professional instruction,
guidance, and demonstration provided by the extension services of
the Israel Ministry of Agriculture and by a resulting recourse of
area farmers to modern techniques and implements. The Director-
General of the Ministry of Agriculture has reported:

> So we moved to Stage Three: development—new seeds,
> intensive market gardening with the aid of irrigation,
> the use of supports for crops like tomatoes, better
> cattle strains. . . .

The guiding line in development is to abandon low-
price produce, like melons, seek new markets and switch
to items for which these markets show a demand.

The demand for labor in Israel assures employment for some
30,000 workers from the areas each day at wages at least 60 percent
higher, on a net basis, than what they would earn in the administered
areas.

The report of the Research Department of the Central Bank
published in January 1971 comments as follows:

> Economic activity and living standards in the administered
> areas continued to increase rapidly in 1969. The number
> of employed showed a further strong rise—15 percent

over the previous year—while unemployment fell to an
average of 5 percent below the pre-war level. The
Gross National Product advanced by a very substantial
25 percent in real terms, or 23 percent per capita.

The accelerated tempo of economic activity led
to a rapid growth of incomes and a consequent jump
in living standards. Real private consumption went
up by 19 percent, or 17 percent per capita. This
upsurge in the standard of living characterized both
the West Bank (Judea and Samaria) and the Gaza
Strip and Northern Sinai. Private consumption per
capita in Judea and Samaria—which contain 62 percent
of the total population of the administered areas—grew
by approximately 19 percent in real terms, while in
the Gaza Strip and Northern Sinai it rose by 11 percent. These increases brought the average standard
of living in the administered areas to above its level
before the Six-Day War. . . .

The expansion of economic activity has brought
about a rapid rise in incomes and private consumption
and also a sharp increase in imports, notably of consumer goods. In the second half of 1967 commodity
imports totalled approximately IL 65 million, rising
to nearly IL 240 million in 1968 and IL 295 million
in 1969.

These developments are illustrated in Table 27.

The earnings of inhabitants of the areas from work in Israel
almost trebled in 1969, accounting for roughly 30 percent of the increment of their GNP. This trend continued in 1970 with earnings
accounting for some 20 percent of the increment in the GNP. Residents of Judea and Samaria took some 75 percent of those earnings
in 1969 and 1970, with residents of the Gaza Strip and Northern Sinai
taking the remainder.

Although data on industrial output are not available, turnover
figures suggest that activity was also stepped up very briskly in that
sector. Total turnover, excluding oil presses, rose by 36 percent
in 1969 and went further ahead by 10 percent in 1970. Gross investment in the areas doubled in 1969 to IL 77 million, aggregating IL
70 million in 1970; in Judea and Samaria, the figure went up from
IL 25 million to IL 56 million with investments totaling IL 46 million
in 1970 (at 1970 prices), and in the Gaza Strip and Northern Sinai
from IL 11 million to IL 21 million and IL 24 million in 1970.

TABLE 27

GNP and Resources in the Administered
Areas, 1968-70
(at 1970 prices)

	1968	1969	1970	Average Percentage Increase
In IL millions				
GNP	521	633	728	18.2
Total Resources	657	810	864	15.0
In IL per capita				
GNP	554	661	748	16.3
Private Consumption	557	670	717	13.6

Source: Bank of Israel.

The first half of 1970 was equally promising, although the
development proceeded at a slower pace. Product grew by an esti-
mated 15 percent from 1969 to 1970, compared with about 21 percent
from 1968 to 1969, but that rapid advance reflected the recovery from
the low level of 1968, a year still depressed by the war and its aftermath.[1] In 1970, the rate of growth apparently leveled off, although
it was fairly high all the same thanks to the resumption of economic
exchanges with Israel.*

The larger effective demand stimulated, as indeed might have
been theoretically postulated, and helped to narrow the gap between
the primitive and lower economic standards of the areas and the
developed economy of Israel by a leveling up process.

The expansion of economic activity in general and its rising
share in the foreign trade of the areas, more subcontracting by Israeli
producers to firms in Gaza, Judea, and Samaria, the growing

---

*In Israel, real product rose by 7 percent in 1970.

employment in Israel of labor from the areas, not only in construction but also on farms and in factories, and a marked ensuing rise average wages in the areas—all these contributed to lessening the economic disparity, notably so, of course, for inhabitants of the areas working in Israel. Income from employment in Israel was substantial, reflecting both the large number so employed and the higher wages. Exports from the areas to neighboring Arab states were larger in 1969 and the first half of 1970 by about 40 percent.

Effective "external demand" for commodities in the neighboring Arab states and for manpower in Israel substantially accelerated the economic growth of the administered areas. However, external demand by itself would not have sufficed: it was effected by a simultaneous introduction of methods of production in farming and by investment and accumulation, as well as by import of capital.

NOTE

1. See The Economy of the Administration Areas, 1969 (Jerusalem: Bank of Israel Research Department, December); The Economy of the Administered Areas, January-June, 1970 (Jerusalem: Bank of Israel Research Department, June, 1971).

The deeper long-run undercurrents in its economy may mold the
pattern of Israel's political, social, and economic future decisively:
Even if they offer no instant solution to all the manifold and vexing
problems with which the country is confronted, they do augur a progressive transformation of the present economic design.

During the Mandatory period, the controversy with the Mandatory
Administration revolved around the concept of absorptive capacity.
British experts insisted that there was no room here "to swing a cat"
and that the economic capacity of absorption of immigration was rigidly
limited or altogether nonexistent. When the 1931 census was taken,
the country was peopled by 175,000 Jews and 795,000 non-Jews, a
total of less than a million. Today, in an Israel occupying only 76
percent of the Mandatory territory, there are 3 million inhabitants
with standards of living and of consumption incomparably higher than
in the 1931 population with its overwhelming majority subsisting on the
primitive Arab standard of living.

The British experts used a virtually "physiocratic "approach, in
the main predicating the country's ability to support its population on
physical area, a static fertility of the soil and the paucity of natural
resources. But the initiators of transplantation and economic growth
were convinced that the importance and weight of natural conditions
in the world economy are progressively declining and that the more
specifically humanly controlled factors of know-how and skill, of
ability and human material, of dedication to a cause, of the level of
education, as well as the import of capital, are becoming more and
more determinant, a changeover accentuated in Israel by a mass
immigration and massive capital inflow. They argued that, with the
expansion of international trade and lower freights, the future of
industrial development, particularly of processing plants in which

raw materials play a subsidiary part, would turn on the dynamics of economic planning, economic policy, the quality of the population, and the investment of capital. Raw materials can be imported and the freight differential is not big enough, especially in the so-called growth industries, which are sophisticated and science-based with little need for raw materials, to interfere with their expansion.

Even in the agricultural sector, physical area is gradually becoming less significant. Farming is on the threshold of a revolution wrought by applying more intensive methods of cultivation and concentrating on specialized crops intended predominantly for export, and extensive farming can also increase its crops by modern agrotechnical methods.

A multiplied population and its higher standards of living and of consumption have vindicated this forecast as against the predictions of the British experts, and the economic trends and tendencies that brought about the metamorphosis are no less in operation today, and with greater vigor. They may be summarized as follows:

1. An altered structure of the economy as a concomitant of the process of industrialization.

2. Higher labor productivity realized by mechanization and the use of scientific methods.

3. The agricultural revolution, which paves the way to overcoming the constraints of space, water, and narrow markets.

4. Industrialization, which encounters no limitations of space and is propelled by large-scale investment, know-how, and skill.

5. A shift from staple to sophisticated industries based on science and with a high added value.

6. Allocation of a larger proportion of output to export so that the economy is more extensively based on the exchange of goods through international trade and becomes more export-oriented—a precondition of successful development in any small country.

These are all positive indexes. Analysis of the resultant facts and figures, as of the motive trends and tendencies, provides ample evidence that these are realities that have crystallized in the course of time and are slowly reshaping the whole fabric of Israel's economy. These facts should be examined in the light of experience.

DEVELOPMENTS IN ISRAEL'S ECONOMY

Occupational Change

More than any other branch of the economy, agriculture suffers from natural limitations. A high percentage of the population employed on the land points to a backward and primitive structure of national economy. As productivity rises and up-to-date techniques of irrigation, seed selection, fertilizers, and mechanization are brought into play, fewer hands are required for the same, or even a larger, output.

In primitive economies with a lower standard of living, such as India, Pakistan, or Egypt, 50 to 75 percent of the population is occupied in farming. In highly developed countries such as the United States, Great Britain, and the Netherlands, the proportion is 3 to 11 percent. In Israel, the figure was 14 percent in 1951 but by 1969 had dropped to 10.5 percent; in the same spell, the figure of employment in industry rose from 23.6 percent to 24.3 percent, reaching 28.1 percent in 1970.

Higher Productivity Per Worker

Productivity per worker rose steadily during the decade of 1960-69 by an annual average of 6.1 percent; in 1969 it went up by an exceptionally high 7.2 percent, and in 1970 by 6.5 percent.

A.L. Gaathon quotes the following data:

Over the whole period for which we measure real output and factor inputs, namely 1950-1965, real GDP grew at an annual rate of 11 percent. This high rate of growth was connected with the high rate of growth of population and capital stock. But even on a per capita basis Israel ranks high among the countries for which records of recent periods are available, though not as high as for aggregate gross product. [1]

A comparison of growth rates of aggregate and per capita product throws some light on the crucial factor of rising productivity in the overall growth of Israel's economy (see Table 29).

The Agricultural Revolution

Although the percentage of the population engaged in agriculture is less that it was, self-sufficiency in food supply is nearer. Whereas in 1950 only half of Israel's food consumption came out of local

TABLE 28

Product Growth in Selected Countries, 1954-64
(compounded annual rate of exchange, percent)

	Aggregate Product	Product Per Man-Year[a]
Japan	9.6	8.0
Israel[b]	9.9	5.7
Italy	5.6	5.7
Austria	5.4	5.2
France	4.9	4.7
West Germany	6.0	4.5
Norway	3.9	3.6
Denmark	4.1	3.3
Belgium	3.6	3.3
Netherlands	4.5	3.2
United Kingdom	2.7	2.1
United States	3.1	1.8
Canada	3.6	1.3

Note: Figures refer to GDP; countries are ranked by product per man-year.

[a]Israel—per employed person; other countries—per member of labor force.
[b]1955-65.

Source: A.L. Gaathon, Economic Productivity in Israel (New York: Bank of Israel—Praeger Publishers, 1971).

TABLE 29

International Comparison on Growth Rates of
Aggregate and Per Capita Product in the 1960's

Compounded Annual Growth Rate, (percent)	Israel	30 Less Developed Countries	26 More Developed Countries
Product	8.7	5.4	5.0
Population	3.5	2.9	1.4
Per capita product*	5.0	2.5	3.6

Note: Figures refer to 1960-69 for Israel, 1960-67 for other countries.

*The population and per capita product growth rates do not necessarily add to the aggregate product growth rate, since the per capita rate was computed as a quotient.

Source: A. L. Gaathon, Economic Productivity in Israel (New York: Bank of Israel—Praeger Publishers, 1971), p. 173.

production, in the late 1960's as much as 85 percent were of local origin and only 15 percent of the country's foodstuffs imported. Meanwhile, the population had more than doubled but the standard of nutrition was much higher. The argument underlying the thesis that economic absorptive capacity must be extremely limited was related to the small area of the country and the consequent dearth of farmland. The thesis that on the same area much larger quantities of food can be produced has been completely vindicated: thus, the yield of wheat per acre rose, taking an average, by more than 100 percent from 1949 to 1967, through more efficient use of water, seed selection, and fertilizers. That is not an isolated example. Milk yield per cow in Israel is the highest in the world, and the output of cotton per acre exceeds that in the United States. So, by the application of know-how, technology, and capital as substitutes for land, limitations of space are neutralized. Marketing frontiers also are receding rapidly: already, exports of citrus top the $100 million mark, five times what they were at the end of World War II, in which groves were badly damaged.

No less important are the new export crops. Shipments of fresh fruit, vegetables, and flowers to Europe during the off-season rose by 77 percent between 1968 and 1970 and, according to the agricultural plan, should in the early 1970's gain a place comparable to that of citrus if the climatic advantages of Israel are exploited and cultivation under cover or in hot-houses is efficiently practiced. This breakthrough in marketing was made possible, in the main, by a readier demand as per capita national income rose in the European centers, allowing more of that national income to be spent on off-season vegetables, fruits, and flowers because of new nutritional habits and attitudes that increase the consumption of vitamins.

Industrialization

The base of industrial production is broadening. The branch naturally benefits from economies of scale. In the years 1968-70, it was tremendously boosted by defense production which, from its spill-over, injected a new technology and know-how into civilian industry. Consequently, factory output advanced in 1968 by 28.6 percent, in 1969 by 17.5 percent, and in 1970 by about 10 percent, among the highest rises in the world. Industrial exports (excluding diamonds) advanced correspondingly—by 29.2 percent in 1968, by 17.5 percent in 1969, and by 13.7 percent in 1970—and they are expected to increase by some 20-25 percent in 1971 (on the basis of data already available for the first 8 months).

THE SHIFT TO SOPHISTICATED AND SCIENCE-BASED INDUSTRIES

Textiles and foodstuffs have shrunk in relative weight while more complex and sophisticated industries based on know-how and with high added value have expanded on a scale far exceeding the average for industry as a whole. Production of electrical and electronic equipment in 1968 was 70 percent over the previous year's level while the comparable figure for machinery was 44 percent and that of metal products, 38 percent; in 1969, the respective figures were 61, 19, and 21 percent. The same trend is manifest in exports: total industrial exports in 1970 (again excluding diamonds) were about 14 percent higher than in 1969, the metal industry registered a gain of 17.2 percent, and electrical and electronic equipment gained 39 percent.

The Growing Export-Orientation of the Economy

In any small country, export-orientation is essential because large-scale production means more efficient production, and it is exceptionally important for Israel, which is low in natural resources and high in standards of living. Without export-orientation, economic development will be hamstrung by balance of payments constraints. In the Netherlands, 42 percent of the GNP is exported. In Israel, exports took no more than 15.2 percent of GNP in 1959, rising, however, to 29 percent in 1970.

OBSERVATIONS

These pages have sought to clarify how the economy of Israel went forward under the impulsion of transplantation, immigration, and abounding investment, which brought a domestic market into being and speeded expansion. But investments are now maturing and the domestic market is saturated. Balance of payment difficulties reveal the weaknesses of an inward-looking economy: it proves too narrow and, if it is to grow; a reorientation outward becomes imperative. That means exports and penetration into world markets.

For a small country, this second stage of development, reversing the first, may be helped along by far-reaching specialization. If that succeeds, even in minor but sophisticated branches of industrial production, the necessarily restricted scope of the units of production need not prevent them from enjoying the advantage of comparative costs since they can find sufficient demand even in the narrow crevices of the world markets.

These six developments mark a progressive emancipation from natural conditions, the greater impact of technology and know-how, the growing importance of the human element. In their dependence upon skill and competence, on the proliferation of institutions of higher learning, and on a high general level of education, these developments parallel global trends, opening up new vistas and wide horizons, provided that the complex and serious but short-run difficulties with which Israel's economy is confronted can be overcome.

The country has been undergoing fundamental modifications of structure. Step by step, it is becoming more of a seller's and a producer's environment. The interests of investor, importer, and consumer are no longer the exclusive consideration. The reason is fairly obvious. The capital imported in the past was used to enlarge productive capacity. The investments are now maturing, production has effactually expanded, and exports have begun to rise steadily. This maturing of earlier capital intake has been accompanied by a growing diversification of export trade. Therefore, the very essence of Israel's economic life and problems is being transformed.

NOTE

1. A. L. Gaathon, Economic Productivity in Israel (New York: Bank of Israel—Praeger Publishers, 1971).

12

Under difficult conditions, sustained growth has been achieved in Israel, reflected in the annual average increment of the GNP by some 10 percent in real terms and a rise in exports in those first twenty years from $46 million to $1,315 million. In 1949, only 14 percent of imports were covered by income from exports; in 1970, the proportion was 51 percent. In 1949, a population of less than a million was supplied by locally produced foodstuffs up to 50 percent; in 1970, for a population of three million the figure was over 85 percent. In 1949, import of capital, or the excess of imports over exports, represented from 40 to 50 percent of total resources; in 1966, the figure was 10.5 percent, and even under near-war conditions in 1970, when military supplies inflated the import bill, the deficit in the balance of payments did not exceed 20 percent of total resources.

Progress, as thus exemplified, was not only quantitative. It changed Israel's economic structure fundamentally.

The rates of growth given are averages, and a high average is always attainable if the start is from a low point: in the first few years, very rapid growth is possible and then the curve flattens out. This was not so in Israel - the rate of growth was sustained with rare interruptions.

What then are the factors making for prosperity at a high level for two decades? It seems that the one that matters most in the emergence and persistence of boom conditions, with a brief intermission of two years, was the continuously rising demand that followed the influx of immigrants and capital. Effective demand had no chance to flag since it was constantly reinvigorated from abroad. The import of capital financed not only investment but also, to a considerable extent, consumption. In fact, production lagged behind purchasing power.

The demand was to some extent a function of internal forces, generated by income distribution, the propensity to consume, and investment. However, it was also and to an even greater extent a function of external forces. Admittedly, the exceptional circumstances of Israel have not been recreated elsewhere to test the validity of this inference, but it is valid just the same, as two decades of economic growth bear out. The inflationary effect of the injection of new purchasing power from overseas, and of the dimensions of investment, was in essence similar to the results of organized public and relief works in other countries. But the buoyancy of demand was not achieved in Israel by planning. It was the spontaneous outcome of the transfer of powerful economic factors from one place to another for partly noneconomic reasons.

It was mass immigration that started the course for a sudden expansion of demand, influx of capital, and diffusion of capital through building activity, and that provided the incentive and momentum for establishing an apparatus of production on the basis of new marketing outlets. Thence, the dynamic growth of the economy.

If the rapidity of that growth, full employment, and certain other economic indicators are analyzed, the evidence is conclusive that the experiment was effective. To understand the phenomenon, a comparison with the background of world development in the nineteenth century is apt. At that time, economic growth in the metropolis, which was Western Europe, was remarkably swift, as was the growth of primary production in the colonial and semicolonial territories. It was an economy of growing population that, invigorated by an enormous industrialization, could absorb everything that the underdeveloped countries produced. New types of colonization—territories such as the British Dominions—attracted emigrants, were producing food, raw materials and primary products, and found a ready market for them in the industrializing West.

World War II ended all that. The problem of overproduction in almost every foodstuff, and raw material and a slowing up of growth in countries of primary production became urgent. That was a characteristic of the great crisis in the 1920's and 1930's. The predicament was aggravated by technological developments, by the substitution of synthetic fibers in place of cotton, artificial rubber in place of natural, plastics in place of wood, and so on. It was the

slump in the prices of primary products that halted the era of colonization. There was a temporary suspension of the process of bringing
people to a colony to produce primary goods for the outside market,
evolve their own economy, and afterward diversify it by industrialization, in that way developing secondary and tertiary stages of production and becoming a self-sufficient unit. Before World War II,
one or two renewed attempts were made with lavish investment of
capital. Italy tried the process in Abyssinia, Somalia, and Libya;
all the ventures failed. Japan, a country of outstanding efficiency,
sank a vast amount of capital in Manchuria; that experiment also was
abortive and most of the settlers returned home because there was
no market for their products. Colonization, in fact, became more a
problem of markets than of production because diversification was
now indispensable: no country—or colony—could viably be established
and profitably developed on the sole strength of primary production
for the markets of the world.

But two successes were registered, and the contention is that
they were successes not of colonization but of transplantation. In
one, there was a transfer of population from Asia Minor to Greece,
which suddenly increased the population of that country by a third.
In the other, Israel has more than trebled its population since 1948.
Here the inverse of the thesis that immigration is a function of economic conditions in the country of absorption is true: economic conditions become a function of immigration. Building and public works
in Israel were a natural outcome of the comigration of capital and
men. They were the spark that ignited a general process of expansion,
tiding the newcomers over the transition period until their integration
in the country, a lever for all other forms of activity. Added purchasing power and new demand thereafter quickened the development
of secondary and tertiary stages of production. The synchronization
of effective demand, financed as it was by capital import, is one of
the reasons, with the growth of production, for Israel's rapid development. Capital imports were substantial and ready to avail themselves
of all prospects for profitable investment, given a market. A constant flow of immigration with increasing real income guaranteed the
market, and capital was invested in the production that was necessary
to meet the growing demand.

It is certainly the case in most underdeveloped countries that
the speed of demographic growth retards economic growth and is an
obstacle to a rise in standards of living. Therefore, if demography
is to be a stimulant of economic growth, a unique breakthrough,
effected by a massive influx of capital, availability of skills, and
institutional and entrepreneurial initiative and ability, must be predicated. Otherwise, a rapidly rising population does not exert a
positive influence on economic growth. Transplantation creates the

internal market that permits a diversified economy and, paradoxically, provides a kind of "external demand" generated by the investment sector.

If, then, immigration to Israel was impelled by noneconomic forces, by a seemingly perilous series of undulations, this was really a blessing in disguise. The end result was a dynamic balance and in the ensuing phase of economic growth there are some universal implications.

After World War I, depression in Europe was ubiquitous. The one country that prospered was France, ruined though it had been in the long war. For the widespread devastation called for reconstruction and reconstruction gave rise to new, countrywide demand and so to prosperity—paradoxical but factual.

Keynes stated:

> It would be worthwhile economically, because of the
> multiplier effect, to set men and machines to work even
> to dig profitless holes in the ground, preferably in the
> most complicated technological way.

Therefore, the theory of economic growth as a product of transplantation is founded on the Keynesian conception: there is an immense potential of production in modern economies and modern technology: balance is made possible by disturbance, equilibrium by disequilibrium.

In the initial period of economic growth, the building industry could rely on a cumulative demand constantly refreshed by immigration and capital inflow. Thus, the starting expansion was based on branches that met no marketing difficulties and in due course made it feasible to expand production for the domestic market. Of course, this chain of reinforcement after reinforcement of demand by recurrences of immigration, construction, and import of capital has its limits, but at the outset of structural development full employment can be achieved and will continue for a good length of time.

In terms of twentieth century economics, what is called pump-priming is in wide application; transplantation is one form of it, and Israel is a case in point. Transplantation triggers off an internal boom in the same way as does an armaments race or a war or the reconstruction that follows a war.

The marked prosperity of West Germany after World War II is in large measure a reflex of the entry of a multitude of refugees from

East Germany. The same is true of Hong Kong, where refugees from mainland China enlarge demand and develop the economy into conditions of boom and full employment.

The central aspect of Israel's development is that entire communities have been transplanted to the country and firmly installed, with all the prerequisites of capital, manpower, and skill, as well as the purchasing power out of which an internal market is born. The elements of economic growth were introduced from different parts of the world; the dynamic reaction of the country's economy to the migratory movement liberated new economic forces.

If transplantation is sufficiently voluminous and rapid and does not peter out into a slow and staggered infiltration, it produces a dynamic equilibrium in which imbalances are overcome by the process of growth which itself opens up new possibilities for absorption, becoming more important than either space or natural resources. However, it would be a fallacy to assume that, to achieve prosperity, it suffices to move people from one place to another. There is a very rapid increment of population in certain underdeveloped nations but their standards of living are deteriorating and they are not affluent by any means. The missing ingredient is an influx of capital corresponding to the human influx. Only a combination of the two and, if possible, an optimum ratio, can result in rapid and sustained economic growth.

What counts in economic growth is, first of all, skill and know-how, then capital, and lastly, natural resources. All three are interchangeable, and so Israel made up for a scarcity of natural resources by more of the other two constituents, namely capital, and skill and know-how, which it could command given an immigration under the thrust of extra-economic motivations. There was no alternative to that form of compensation if the twofold transformation of country and people was to be realized. But the factor of imponderables cannot be ignored. Of this precondition of rapid economic growth, John Kenneth Galbraith stated:

One country that has shown great advance since the war, including great capacity to make effective use of aid, has been Israel. It is singularly unendowed with natural resources. It has no oil wells, few minerals, insufficient water and not much space. But all the four elements mentioned—a highly educated élite, the sense and the reality of social justice, an effective government and a strong sense of purpose are all present. So there is a rapid progress. The Israelis, were they forced to it, would better do without their aid than without their

education, their sense of shared responsibility and
shared gains, their public administration and their clear
view of their destiny.

Skill and know-how, vital as they are, can in no way be considered the only quality of human resources that has been at work in
Israel. Social and economic versatility and flexibility, the ability
of adaptation to new and changing circumstances, are an essential
precondition of rapid economic growth. An economy established in
a new and exacting environment by a very diversified immigrant
population, with the processing of imported raw materials integral
to its progress, requires a high rate of productivity and competitiveness on international markets. Modernization of enterprises and a
change in the composition of production factors and the pattern of
economic development are essential in such circumstances. Shifts
of resources, capital, and labor presuppose an unusual degree of
adaptability and mobility in all elements of growth.

Progress in managerial skills, a willingness to try out new
processes and technologies and new methods of marketing, pioneering
in experimentation and in structural reform—all these have demonstrated their fertility and effectiveness. In an economy as fluid and
dynamic as Israel's, in the second half of the twentieth century with
scientific innovation and discovery no longer a monopoly of major
states, a manpower that is receptive to novelty and change is the
most precious asset of any country, regardless of size. For a contemporary, dynamic economy in constant readjustment, the determining factors are intelligence and initiative, motivation and flexibility,
and these are qualities that could only be acquired in a closely-knit
society with a strong sense of solidarity that overrides its multiple
diversity, and with a common denominator of national and social
aspirations. These attributes could hardly have been effectual were
it not for the singular conditions of transplantation.

The geographical transfer of segments of Israels' population
from over a hundred countries is a one-time operation. But the social
and economic absorption and integration of these immigrants is a
protracted process: the first is a logistic task for which transport
and housing are needed; the second is the heart of the economic
problem of Israel.

At the present juncture, it is plain that, now that the physical
framework of the economy has been constructed in the first two
decades, it should be possible to utilize productive capacity for
economic emancipation. Rising exports, reduced imports, and more
saving for investment should by degrees lessen the gap in the balance
of payments and, at the end of the third decade the economy should be

self-supporting with import of capital serving for its further expansion. In the first two decades of its working, and that in the most trying of conditions, this policy has yielded results that, considering the difficulties of the period, should be indicative of future prospects.

The problems and difficulties with which Israel was confronted in its economic growth were as formidable as its achievements. The gravest and most stubborn problem is endemic and persistent inflation; rampant in the first years of independence because of monetary expansion and budgetary deficits, inflation still persists, if in milder form. The diversion of very large resources to defense requirements is another element in this equation.

In the first period of Israel's statehood, until the first monetary reform of 1952, inflation reflected budgetary deficits and monetary expansion. In those four years, prices rose by 114 percent and means of payment by 217 percent. Under the pressures of an unprecedented immigration that doubled the population, burdensome defense expenditures, and rapid economic growth, monetary expansion was bound to be rapid since the normal means of financing the flood of immigrants and their economic integration fell short of needs. It was a kind of war economy in which unorthodox financial methods led inevitably to runaway inflation, depletion of foreign currency reserves, and physical shortages. The geopolitical and military backgrounds are permanently adverse factors since the heavy outlay on arms is a continuing drain on resources.

The monetary reform in 1952 was relatively successful. A policy aimed at equilibrium was instituted. Immigrants were not as numerous. Now began a period of creeping inflation in which the rise of prices was less pronounced. In the years 1952 and 1953, means of payment kept expanding at an annual rate of 17.3 percent and prices at an average rate of 6.5 percent. The sources of this expansion, although much more moderate and on a smaller scale, were as before: deficit financing of state budgets and credit expansion. Absorption of an unintegrated backlog of immigration, the cost of security, and continuing economic progress combined to increase state expenditure, and bank credit went up at an average annual rate of 15.8 percent.

Inflationary pressures showed themselves in the consumer price index, which rose on the average by 9.9 percent per year in the two decades. In the 1960's inflationary pressures were mitigated by reason of the annual growth of the GNP by 10.6 percent and of the excess of imports over exports, aggregating $6.4 billion. However, since 1967 these pressures have increased again as a result of the war.

Throughout, the most striking aspect of this development was
a complete absence of the usual business cycle, except for the two
years 1965-66. It was a oneway traffic: however, dynamic growth
and inflationary pressures with their harmful effects were seldom
lacking. The deficit budgeting of the state, which was responsible
for the early inflation, represented an attempt to raise additional
funds for development through "inflationary saving." But here, with
hardly any dormant factors of production in existence that could be
galvanized by monetary expansion and deficit financing, a point was
very soon reached at which bottlenecks prevented expansion of production beyond the average annual rate, already high by any criterion.
Monetary expansion overstepping that mark led to rising prices and
a very adverse balance of payments.

Rapid economic growth and full employment resulted in an overheated economic activity, a super-boom. The economy was plagued
by four excesses: overliquidity, overconsumption, overinvestment,
and overemployment with a shortage of labor in its wake. The large
state development budget and private investment poured more projects
and money into the economy than available physical factors of production could handle. The rise in incomes necessarily resulting
from boom conditions and full employment exerted new inflationary
pressures. With economic activity already overheated, the import
of capital, while still desirable, could only mean further monetary
expansion and imported inflation.

Mention has been made of the forces countervailing these powerful stimuli and incentives. By a restrictive monetary, fiscal, and
incomes policy, the monetary expansion due to imported inflation is
being offset in part. But this policy coincides head-on with the traditional tenacious aspirations and inclinations of the public, un-
swervingly intent on developing, prepared to favor any tempo of
activity and progress and to see it encouraged and pressed on whatever the circumstances. On the other hand, the rapid rise in standards of living and consumption, which is substantiated by statistical
data showing a declining share of food in total expenditure and increased purchases of durable consumer goods and of services in the
past few years, * has itself provided the necessary conditions for the
policy of counteracting inflationary pressures generated by large-
scale import of capital, without inflicting too much hardship on the
population.

_____

*See Chapter 3.

Israel has a surplus in the overall balance of payments but a
very adverse current balance. Imports exceeded exports in the years
1966-70 as follows: by $440 million in 1966, by $532 million in 1967,
by $718 million in 1968, by $894 million in 1969, and by $1, 265 million
in 1970, all including war imports. If progress toward economic
emancipation and independence from foreign aid is to be measured
by balance of payments, the adverse current balance will have to be
put right after a period of hectic development on the strength of a
massive import of capital.

The situation must be viewed in the context of prospects for
the balance of payments. Lack of foreign currency would make matters
difficult because it might not only curtail imports of consumer goods
but also affect production through shortage of raw materials, fuel,
and so on, in which eventuality unemployment and physical dearths
could not be prevented.

The time lag between investment and its maturing must also
be reckoned with. Since the sources of foreign aid that help forward Israel's economic growth are likely to dwindle in the course of
time, their place must be filled by a rise in GNP, which means win-
ning the race against time. Some progress toward that aim can be
recorded. First, while the total excess of imports over exports
went up from $282 million in 1950 to $445 million in 1966 (the last
year before the Six-Day War which, of course, made it go up a great
deal more), the deficit in the trade balance per capita dropped from
$222 to $169 in the same period.

It is obvious that the balance of trade can be further improved
only by an expansion of exports. Against their growth from $46
million in 1950 to $832 million in 1966 must be set a concurrent rise
in imports. It is a matter of competitive capacity, of gaining permanent entry into world markets. With rapid physical expansion
in full stride, the achieving and maintaining of that capacity were to
some extent neglected and inflation was tolerated for too long.

Like most of the world's small countries, Israel is under the
necessity of allocating much of its resources to exports. Small
countries understandably are more dependent on foreign trade than
states that are rich in natural wealth, although even the biggest are
not altogether self-sufficient. Territories with few raw materials
of their own require a correspondingly larger quantity and wider
variety of imported commodities for their own production. To earn
the foreign currency needed for these acquisitions, they must step
up their exports so as to ensure full employment and self-sustained
growth of their economies. Exports are thus inseparable from the
objective of continuing production and employment because they

finance the means of procuring the import component without which
the economy would run down and unemployment spread. In this context, Israel's competitive capacity is crucial.

It appears that the main further rise in Israel's exports will be
to the developed countries, which absorbed about 83 percent of Israel's
exports in 1970. Israel's farm produce, grown in a subtropical
climate, evidently is not marketable in countries with similar climatic
conditions but sells well in temperate zones.

Except for the minerals in the Dead Sea, Israel has few raw
materials. Consequently, local manufacture must concentrate by
and large on processing, utilizing imported raw materials and exporting the finished products. Israel's contribution in skill, labor,
and capital, as is the case for Switzerland and Holland, lends itself
to the polishing of diamonds and to the manufacture of chemicals,
fine metal instruments, and electrical and electronic appliances.
The markets are to be found in countries with high incomes and developed industries.

Production on a minor scale for its own population of three
million cannot be profitable, and artificial growth under a protective
tariff would drag Israel out of the orbit of world economic trends
and distort its industrial pattern. The very thrust of an expanding
economy was aided by the world-wide shift from material to human
resources as the most important agents of economic growth.

The many dynamic, powerful, and contradictory trends and
tendencies to which Israel's economy is exposed are disconcerting,
at times seemingly intractable. If development is to be balanced, if
the dynamism is to be preserved yet confined securely within a
framework of stability and equilibrium, unpopular policies must be
followed. The excess in per capita consumption and standards of
living must be checked if the external payments account is to be
squared, and the meagerness of internal savings redressed if investment is to gradually become independent of unilateral transfers of
capital. A balanced budget, a wages and incomes policy aimed at
restraint, and a stringent limitation of credits are the only instruments for the purpose. The government's incomes, fiscal, and
monetary policies pursuing these ends are bound to run counter to
popular pressures and wishes, so that, within the economy of a state
under geopolitical conditions of veritable siege and isolation, clash
and conflict cannot be avoided. And yet, the salient objective of
Israel's economic program, in its planning and performing, is to
sustain economic development in a democratic regime, despite
geopolitical handicaps.

The circumstance that most of the large import of capital into Israel comes from public and semipublic sources and is channeled into the economy through the government or such public institutions as the Jewish Agency has been instrumental in developing a large sector of public and semipublic economic undertakings in agriculture, industry, transport, building, and virtually every other branch. Investment by the state through its development budget or by public institutions is impossible, to all intents and purposes, without planning and a proper order of priorities. Official policy and local exigencies, as well as the need to build a bridge to world markets, join forces in fostering a general tendency toward economic liberalization, but in the conjuncture described—of public and semipublic undertakings, of planning and priorities—such a policy encounters serious difficulties.

Moreover, the socioeconomic structure is exceptionally diversified. Governmental, private and cooperative labor sectors coexist in a kind of symbiosis in an economy where the governing political objectives of the state must come first. The investment of immense amounts of public capital in itself prepares the ground for the emergence of a form of mixed economy. It is too early to judge the success of the experiment, but it can already be discerned that the philosophy behind the maze of cross-currents is pragmatic, a function of the conditions of Israel's economy and society, producing a new socioeconomic morphology of differing elements in a reciprocity of adjustment and accommodation.

Effective demand must be the primary stipulation. Next, modern technology, which permits a degree of independence of natural resources. Then public capital is required in volume to establish the infrastructure, especially at the start.

But plainly the process cannot be projected ad infinitum. A second limiting factor is demography: there must be a high proportion of skills in the population. A third, particularly important, is a sizable import of capital to expand productive capacity and step up effective internal demand at the outset. A fourth is a steady rise in productivity so that exports can be competitive on world markets, a goal for which it is clear that much of the economy must work if the balance of payments is to reach an equilibrium.

An economy cannot be established merely by taking in each other's washing, but, as the experience of Israel thus far suggests, transplantation, subject to many reservations, can obtain some positive results. This conception is predicated on certain preconditions:

1. There must be comigration: a simultaneous influx of man-power and capital.

2. Transplantation must be in large numbers and each tide of it condensed within a short period of time.

3. An occupational reshuffle, a high quality of human material, and an extra-economic propellant are indispensable.

4. Transplantation cannot permanently solve the problems of a modern economy but it can establish a temporary equilibrium for long enough to expand the existing economy or build a new one.

In this transplantation, the contradictions inherent in modern economy will be reproduced to an extent that a variety of economic and material conditions determines, but there is no a priori reason why, when the process of rapid expansion ends, they should be more perplexing or pronounced than if transplantation had not taken place. The effectiveness of transplantation is to be ascribed to the emergence of an economy of a growing population endowed with the requisites of production, capital, skill and knowledge, and systematically inter-changing capital and skill with natural resources. This substitution made for expanded production in step with a widening of the internal market, a rise in productivity and modernization. Experience—brief though it admittedly is—of the slowing down of transplantation-expansion scarcely justifies an assumption that the transplanted body is particularly sensitive or vulnerable.

On the whole, there were three principal elements in the pattern of economic activity, growth, and development of Israel, but their interaction renders it difficult to disengage their respective impacts and influences or to measure their relative weights. These three elements are as follows: (1) the exogenous impulses—immigration, influx of capital, regional political and military developments, and global economic movements; (2) the immanent forces of Israel's economy in their reaction to exogenous impulses and the economic cycle of prosperity and depression thereby set in motion; and (3) the bearing of the economic policy of the government and public institutions on internal and exogenous factors alike.

The high level of immigration and investment buttressed the security of the state, raised the standard of living, and contributed to social and political stability. But the price of economic and extra-economic gains was high. If a balance sheet of economic policy were drawn up, it undoubtedly would show success in quickening economic growth at a pace almost without precedent. On the other hand, containment of inflationary pressures was less successful since

too many objectives were sought at once: the disparity between
monetary expansion, with excessive growth of money supply and
credit, could not be set off by an increment of real resources, and
repercussions on the level of prices and the balance of payments
were inevitable. Surpluses in the overall balance of payments intensified inflation; overliquidity, overinvestment, overemployment,
and overconsumption followed; the whole pattern of the economy
was distorted. The intense activity and development and the countercyclical policy of the government raised standards of living, built
up the security of the state, and advanced economic growth, but
they were equally the generators of insistent political and social
pressures.

This all constitutes an experiment in rapid economic growth
and in restraint of inflation, in expansion under democracy, in controls juxtaposed with liberalization, in a polymorphia of socioeconomic
forms. The experiment takes place in a little country within a short
period of time. Much has been creditably accomplished, many hur-
dles have yet to be crossed.

The state and people of Israel are confronted with many difficult
problems: the takeoff to self-sustaining economic growth, an equilibrium in the balance of payments, the control of inflation, the diversity
of a heterogeneous socioeconomic structure, and geopolitical isolation.
The result of their endeavors may allow the drawing of some more
universal conclusions applicable to economic growth from the events
that have transpired in the diminutive national unit of Israel.

ABOUT THE AUTHOR

DAVID HOROWITZ, Governor of the Bank of Israel from 1954 to 1971 and now Chairman of the Bank's Advisory Committee and Advisory Council, was born in Poland and received his education in Vienna and Lwow. He settled in Palestine in 1920 and served in such capacities as economic advisor, university lecturer, Director of the Economic Department of the Jewish Agency, and member of the delegation to the United Nations.

Upon the establishment of the State of Israel, Mr. Horowitz was appointed Director General of the Ministry of Finance. In his capacity as the Governor of the Bank of Israel, he headed many missions to various meetings of international financial and economic bodies. He has been member of the Boards of Governors of the Hebrew University, Tel Aviv University, and other scientific institutions.

Mr. Horowitz was awarded the Israel Prize for Social Sciences. In 1967, the Hebrew University bestowed upon him the title of doctor honoris causa in recognition of his scientific and public achievements. The same title was bestowed upon him by the Tel-Aviv University in 1970.

Mr. Horowitz is the author of the well-known Horowitz Plan for the financing of the development of underdeveloped nations recommended by the United Nations Conference on Trade and Development in 1964. Apart from his extensive economic and political activities, Mr. Horowitz is also widely known for his many studies and books published in Israel and abroad. Among these are: Economic Survey of Palestine, 1938; State in the Making, 1953; World Economic Disparities, 1962; Hemispheres North and South, 1966; The Economics of Israel, 1967; The Abolition of Poverty, 1969; Ha-etmol Sheli (My Yesterday), 1970.